A desire to end personal suffering arose.
It became clear that inquiry
was the way to end it.
It was understood that inquiry
is learned by inquiring.
And that all thinking
is utterly useless.
Inquiries were found
that resonated.
Expectations about results
were ignored.
Inquiry did me.
I had nothing to do with it.

SEEING NO-SELF

SEEING NO-SELF

ESSENTIAL QUESTIONS TO REVEAL OUR NONDUAL NATURE

Katrijn Van Oudheusden

Hierophant publishing

Cover design by Adrian Morgan
Cover art by chyworks | Shutterstock
Print book interior design by Frame25 Productions

Hierophant Publishing
San Antonio, TX
www.hierophantpublishing.com

If you are unable to order this book from your local bookseller, you may order directly from the publisher.

Library of Congress Control Number: 2025950112
ISBN: 978-1-950253-77-7

10 9 8 7 6 5 4 3 2 1

Contents

This is the paradoxical freedom
that comes from knowing
beyond doubt that

a) this life is a dream, and
b) we do not have an ounce of freedom in *the dream.*

Suffering is believing the dream
is real and that there's freedom to be
found within it.

Real freedom is waking up to
the dream to enjoy it
no matter what its content.

Foreword

If you have picked up this book, you are likely on a journey to discover your true nature—or are at least curious about the profound meaning of "no-self."

In either case, you have found the right guide.

Katrijn Van Oudheusden's *Seeing No-Self* serves as a wise sherpa, leading you on the most significant adventure there is: the exploration of your own existence.

This book is a collection of exercises designed to guide you beyond conceptual understanding and into direct experience. While the mind loves to analyze, truth is revealed not through thought, but through immediate, unfiltered awareness. These practices are masterfully tailored for the contemporary seeker, offering a direct path to the peace that our overactive minds so desperately need.

A skilled guide, Van Oudheusden knows the importance of preparation. She first sets the stage, gently dissolving the very expectations that can block our seeing.

There is nothing new to acquire here, for your true nature is already and always present. This book does not add anything; it simply helps you remember what has been forgotten. The exercises are not goals to achieve, but a gentle reminder of what you already are.

In this light, the practices themselves become the teacher, and the "student" you believed yourself to be begins to dissolve. Once engaged, these explorations become a touchstone—something you can return to again and again, using direct experience to plumb ever-greater depths.

And the book doesn't end there, as the author thoughtfully includes a final section on integrating this understanding into daily life. The realization of no-self is not an esoteric escape; it is the most practical way to end suffering for ordinary people. So, read this book, but more importantly, do the exercises. You have nothing to lose except the persistent, and ultimately illusory, idea of who you thought you were.

—Chris Niebauer, PhD

Author of *No Self, No Problem: How Neuropsychology Is Catching Up to Buddhism*

Preface

Writing books about nonduality is a constant struggle between the mind thinking it can't be done and it happening anyway. That you're reading this is proof that life unfolds through the body-mind and the illusory self has nothing to say about it!

Nondual inquiry is even more difficult to write about, because (a) we're describing something that takes place beyond the mind, and (b) what inquiry needs to be is dependent on the background of the inquirer. Even the language that is most effective depends on the individual. Nevertheless, this book is my best attempt at describing what most of us need to see to realize our true nature.

Like the other books I have written, this book emerged because I couldn't find the book I wanted: in this case, a short, practical book with essential inquiries on nonduality. The goal for this book is to provide you with enough information to see no-self. It is not an exhaustive encyclopedia of possible investigation.

In most cases, this book will not reference specific teachers, lineages, or schools, because, as I hope you will soon see, these are just categories that are likely to lead the mind away from the truth of who you really are. Instead, I've included the exact instructions and inquiries that worked for me after more than a decade of searching, and have also worked for the many other seekers I've guided over the years.

This book is written from the premise that if you do the inquiries and investigate deeply, you will see what there is to see. You can't fail. It may take longer than the ego likes. It may seem as though nothing is happening. But eventually, it will be the most obvious thing in the world.

I invite you to inquire until the inquirer dissolves.

Let's be clear: this is not promising a better life.

There is no such thing as a better life.

This is freedom from the drama of life.

The dream goes on, but it's now known to be a dream. All the stress and suffering were about a fictional character. When the dream no longer fools, the dream character dissolves. It is no longer a real entity with problems to solve.

Freedom.

And as a nice little extra:

***You** recognize yourself as everything.*

Part I

Why Inquire?

You Are Welcome

There is no fluff here. I've removed any detours to make this as short as possible. We are going to the recognition of our true nature as directly as we can currently manage using language. You don't need to know anything about nonduality to dive right in. Nonduality is just another concept. Potentially helpful at first, and a potential hindrance later. The less you think you know, the better.

This is a simple guide to an ordinary rediscovery of what **You**[1] already are. We are rediscovering and recognizing something we innocently forgot and lost awareness of as we grew up.

This book is useless if all you do is read it. It's like swimming. You don't learn how to swim from a manual. You must jump in the pool. This is all about the inquiries and investigations. Nothing about nonduality is useful unless it is a lived understanding. That means it's no longer just a concept. You have seen it for yourself and have no further doubts that it is true.

We will start with a reminder of why inquiry is helpful and how it works. Then I'll share some tips on how to inquire—you've got to stop thinking and look.

---

1. In this guide, I use **You** to refer to our true, nondual nature and *you* to refer to the separate self. Incidentally, describing direct inquiry often requires ignoring rules of grammar.

The thirty-three essential inquiries, placed in a specific, suggested order, form the core of this book. Of course, you can skip the instructions and go straight into the inquiries if you prefer. Finally, we will discuss what happens after inquiry.

If you have questions or get stuck, I suggest finding a human guide for support: there are many experienced guides who have realized what this book is pointing to. There is something about live guidance that is impossible to capture in writing. Similar to the Zen saying "the teaching passes from warm hand to warm hand," this understanding is worth it.

The one searching for its non-existence doesn't exist.
May this bring thinking to a screeching halt.

It's impossible to prove the non-existence of something.

But by looking for the existence of a separate
self, it can be realized, suddenly or slowly, that
there is no self and there is only this.

You *already are what you are seeking.*

Inquiry: What, Why, and How

A nondual understanding is useless unless
it is completely absorbed and lived.

Why Rediscover Our True Nature?

Because **You** are the joyful freedom
of all of this

But you're unhappy
because you believe
you're stuck in one of these,
trying very hard not to mess
up your life

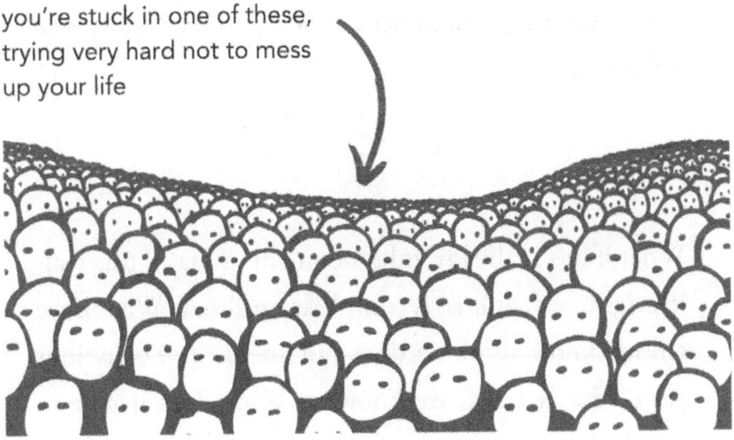

Terminology

This book is titled *Seeing No-Self*. Of course, you can't see the absence of something. It's a paradox. The title could just as easily have been *Seeing Our True Nature*. But it's also impossible to give what we are a name, so we're stuck with bad titles.

Naming our true nature can make it seem like we are another object separate from ourselves, the subject. Whereas the whole point is that we are *one with it*, that *we are it*. It's easier—although still quite challenging—to describe what we're not.

So in this text, I'll use different words to point to our true nature in the hope of not making it too much into a thing. I will also refer to it as Aliveness, Presence, Being, Awareness, Knowing, and **You**. Whenever we refer to what we are, we use capitalization to differentiate it from the separate self, although there is no actual difference.

What if *this* is already enlightenment? What if this reality, right now, as it is, is completely realized? What if we already know all we need to, but are just not conscious yet of the fact that we know it? What does it take to stop being unconscious of something?

All it takes to stop being unconscious is, of course, to become conscious. This consciousness is the only aim of inquiry. There is no guarantee that inquiry will lead to consciousness, but next to hoping for a flash of lightning, it is the most likely method to allow us to see.

We Are the Sky Already

There is no self in the human body. We are animal organisms, human beings, mistakenly believing we are human *selfings* because we've learned to believe in an illusory separate self that supposedly runs the body-mind.

What do you notice in the image below? You probably see an artistic drawing of two clouds. What we normally don't notice is the white space around them. We are obsessed with content and ignore the container.

But essentially, the container is all there is: an eternal, infinite reality *that we are.* We each feel like one small cloud among 8 billion others, but when we look closely we see that we are transparent and insubstantial. There is only endless sky—and we are that sky. We only mistook ourselves for clouds because it's what we learned as children.

What does the sky need to do to realize it is sky? Nothing at all. The only thing required is a recognition of the misidentification. As soon as the sky recognizes itself as sky, the game of being limited to a cloud is up. This also means that the insubstantial cloud can't wake up. It's the sky that wakes up to itself.

A Better Me?

We come to nonduality and inquiry wanting to improve our lives, whether we admit it or not. We believe that understanding will produce a better (more aware) body-mind. But this belief blocks us from noticing what is already here. We assume something needs to happen to us in the future, and constantly overlook what is already aware of everything right now.

Believing something will change for the person keeps us looking ahead, distracting us from the Awareness that's already happening within. What nonduality points to is *this*, as it *already* is. It's already the case *now.*

It's this life exactly as it is. Nothing about the life of the body-mind improves. We don't develop a more aware body-mind: the body-mind is already aware!

Most of us view life through a distorting selfing filter that is invisible to us. But becoming conscious of this filter doesn't remove it—it only makes it visible. It still distorts, but now we can see the distortion and are no longer fooled. The only thing that changes is *belief* in the person-filter. This changes how we experience life. There is a change in *the quality of experience*, not the experience itself.

As we'll see at the end of this book, it's common to not notice the effects of inquiry until we encounter situations we would have resisted or suffered under in the past. Sometimes others point out the effects to us before we notice them.

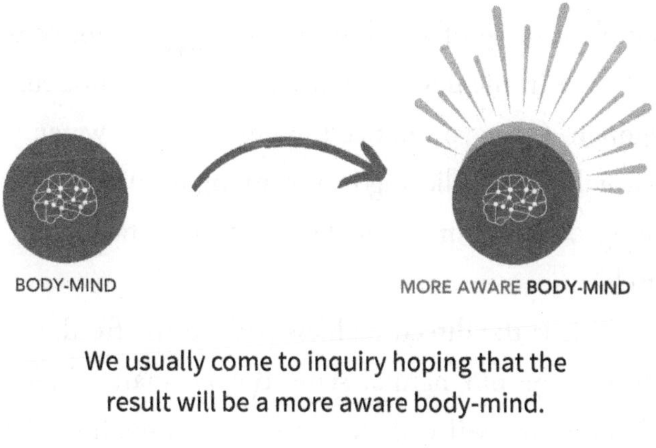

We usually come to inquiry hoping that the result will be a more aware body-mind.

Already the Case

If there is anything to understand from this introduction, it's that the reality this book explores is already the case. This will be repeated ad nauseam because it's so essential. Awakening, enlightenment, true nature, freedom, liberation, realization, no-self . . . it's all already here and perfectly realized. We are just not conscious of it; we innocently believe the story that what we experience with our senses is the only reality!

So, there is nothing to do, nothing to get, nothing to achieve, nothing to make happen, nothing to cultivate, and nothing to deepen. There's no need to do anything at all about this. There's no need to fix our current reality, improve it, or even attempt to escape it. That would be more selfing.

There is only something to see (realize, recognize, notice, be aware of, or become conscious of). This is a simple *noticing* of an illusion, the way you notice that a mirage in the desert is not real water. The noticing is enough. Once you notice the mirage is not water, you naturally stop believing it or running toward it. Everything downstream from the recognition takes care of itself.

This is the direct, pathless path to the freedom we already are: our natural state. But no matter how we phrase it, the self will try to come in through the back door and make that state a goal for it to achieve. (Even not achieving it can become something to achieve!) Just notice this: how the mind makes something—anything—that it can control into a how-to. No matter how much we understand, thinking will always try to control it. That's okay. Just watch the self. Selfing is a natural expression of life. It's just not what we are.

You are not a self. There's only all of *this*, and **You** are *this*.

There Is No Path, and No Person to Walk It

Most spiritual paths aim to free, awaken, or enlighten the self. They are trying to get a seeker to find or experience something so that the seeker will become liberated.

Nonduality and direct inquiry are about discovering the absence of that seeker. If it's a path, it's a pathless path to *no-where*. There is nothing for a fictional seeker to do or gain. There is only a shift of knowing where it's seen that *there is no self* needing freedom. We are already freedom itself.

There's no need to try to create or discover anything new or different. When we realize that there is no us, what is left is everything we were looking for. It was already right there!

However, we often continue to believe that the illusory separate person must go out and develop

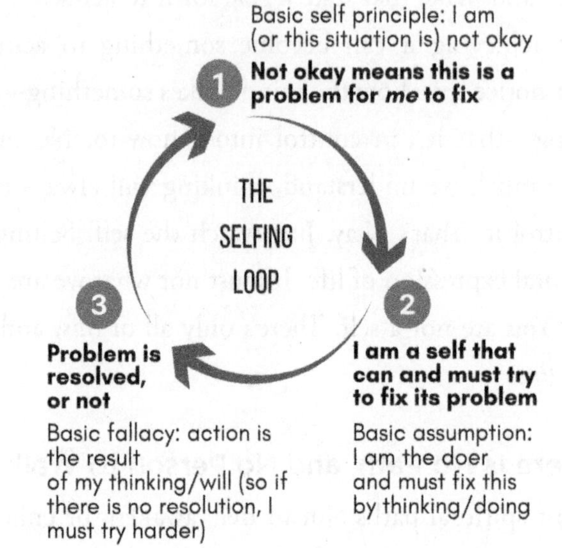
Basic self principle: I am (or this situation is) not okay
1
Not okay means this is a problem for *me* to fix
THE SELFING LOOP
2
I am a self that can and must try to fix its problem
Basic assumption: I am the doer and must fix this by thinking/doing
3
Problem is resolved, or not
Basic fallacy: action is the result of my thinking/will (so if there is no resolution, I must try harder)

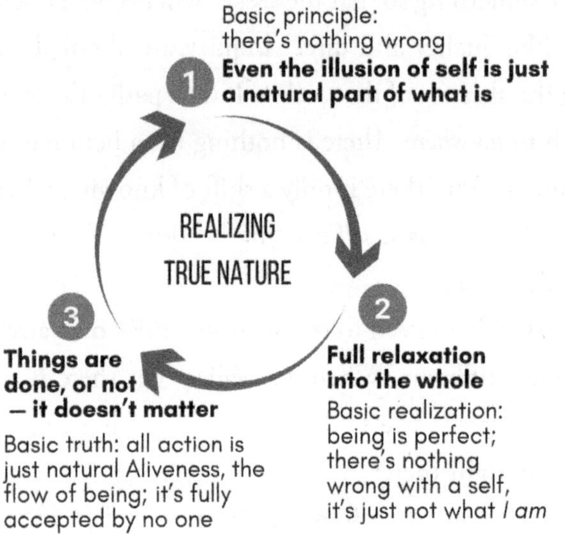
Basic principle: there's nothing wrong
1
Even the illusion of self is just a natural part of what is
REALIZING TRUE NATURE
2
Full relaxation into the whole
Basic realization: being is perfect; there's nothing wrong with a self, it's just not what *I am*
3
Things are done, or not — it doesn't matter
Basic truth: all action is just natural Aliveness, the flow of being; it's fully accepted by no one

themselves. We don't realize that there's no one to do this. We can spend lifetimes on progressive, spiritual paths. Or we can forget about paths altogether and inquire.

Again, this is about discovering that the separate, striving self is a mirage. It looks and feels very real. It's sometimes a useful tool, and it's part of our reality in duality. But we can also see right through it and notice how insubstantial it is. Then who are we protecting, promoting, or trying to improve? If there's no one there, what are we getting so obsessed and upset about?

The same is true for others. Just as there is no real separate self, there are no real separate others. If we get angry at someone, what are we attacking? We assume that there is a separate, autonomous entity in the body we're upset with which is responsible for their behavior. But, as the inquiries will show us, there is no one there.

What remains is We. And this doesn't mean denying that we're separate bodies with individual needs. This is an individual, unique experience with a simultaneous realization of the unity of all existence. Both things are true at once.

The freedom we rediscover is not only *freedom from* life as a separate self. It is then also *freedom as* a self. The self doesn't stop selfing, but we are free from it nonetheless.

Why See No-Self?

You're likely far enough down the nonduality rabbit hole that you no longer need answers to this question. But sometimes reminders are helpful. Here is a list of some benefits of recognizing your freedom from the separate self:

- The sense of disconnection from the world disappears—no more "no one gets me."
- The boundary between you and others fades, unearthing our shared being.
- No more competitive instincts or urges to win at the expense of others.
- Experiencing wholeness, oneness, and integration within life itself.
- A profound trust that makes you feel carried by the entirety of life.
- A natural, unconditional empathy and compassion for others.
- Spontaneous gratitude, awe, and joy for life's simple existence.
- No more stress, worry, or anxiety born out of attempts to control or improve life.

- Freedom from self-judgment, as well as the desire to judge or be judged by others.
- A continuous flow of presence, fully engaged in the here and now.
- A complete acceptance of all life's fluctuations, good and bad.
- An intrinsic desire to serve, in line with your unique gifts.
- Joy that arises regardless of circumstances.
- An unwavering confidence in the expression of life as it unfolds—uncontrived and unshakable.

You are not a person.

You are what is aware of the person (right now, already).

That Awareness (the very same awareness that is aware of the person) is all there ever is, all there ever was, and all there ever will be.

What Is Inquiry?

Nondual inquiry is not a "how-to."
Inquiry is a question: "What-is?"

Peeling Back the Layers

For most, seeing beyond the separate self to our true nature feels like being on a difficult, painful, incremental path. Often, we don't even know where the path is. There are so many options and dead ends. We're trying to navigate a labyrinth in the dark.

The joke is that we already *are* our true nature. Every step we take on any path is a step away from it. We have to stop and look at what we already are right now and forget about a path. There is no path.

The trouble is that our belief in the separate self is in the way of our seeing this. So, in the inquiry, it's important to deconstruct this idea of being a self before we can get a peek into no-self. We have to peel away the layers to see that there's no one there. We also need to ensure we don't become stuck in a nihilistic idea of no-self, but simultaneously rediscover our ever-present Being—our true nature before and beyond any idea of self.

Doing this requires some form of inquiry. You can't get this from books, teachers, or energetic transmissions. You have to take attention off the content of experience and look at what is experiencing all this.

Direct Inquiry

Inquiry is an investigation of direct, first-person experience in the present moment. During this process, we'll look at two things:

1. How *the content of experience* comes and goes, so it can't be what we essentially are. The content includes all of our perceptions, as well as thoughts and sensations.

2. How *the container of experience* (what the content appears within) is always already there: never coming, going, or changing in any way. This leads to the recognition that we can't be the content and must be the container.

The words *content* and *container* are provisional to make an initial distinction. They are only pointing at the truth, so don't try to make sense of them. The inquiries in this book will clarify this.

You may have heard the term *inquiry*, also often called *self-inquiry*, before. This was the term used by the Hindu sage Ramana Maharshi to describe the practice of becoming aware of the sense of *I am* and then abiding as that. In this book, the variations of this essential inquiry are called Awareness Inquiries. They are placed mainly toward the end of the book. But before we get to them, we'll focus on the inquiries investigating what we are not.

Inquiry as presented in this book is not concentration practice, nor is it like Buddhist mindfulness practices you may be familiar with. It isn't a type of reflection, either, because it doesn't involve thinking about anything. It is not a practice in the sense of being an exercise done for an extended period (often many years) at which we become more skilled over time. However, it does require practice!

When reading this book, it's best to forget any ideas you have about inquiry and approach it with a fresh mind.

Inquiry Is Empirical

The beauty of inquiry is that it is rational and empirical—two qualities we tend to value. *Rational* is meant in the sense of not requiring belief, faith, or conviction, rather than in the sense of requiring rational thinking.

Inquiry is empirical because we observe only what is. We gather direct, first-person experience: raw sensations and perceptions only. And we ignore our thoughts about them. So, just as when we were small children, the raw sensory perceptions and data are key. We notice *what is* without consciously adding any beliefs. We try to be as precise as we can. We don't think, intellectualize, or try to understand. We bring all our attention to a direct examination of the empirical facts, much as a detective gathers clues to solve a murder mystery.

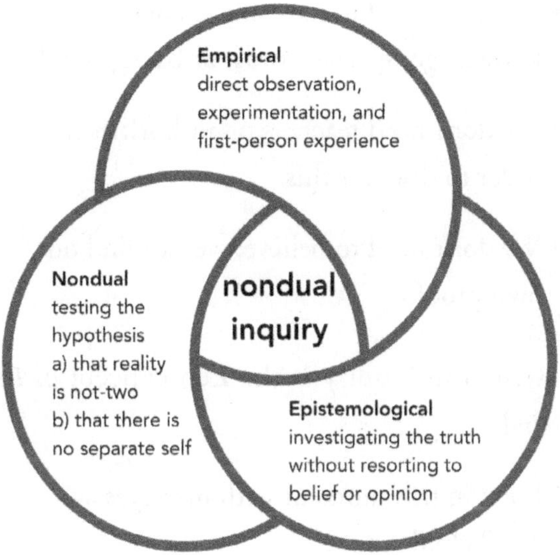

As Simple as Possible

Relax—this is all much simpler than the mind makes it out to be. But you will need to look with fresh eyes and rediscover the innocence and wonder of a child. Forget everything you've learned, including any notion of nonduality and other spiritual concepts. Be careful of the mind's tendency to take yourself or this search too seriously. Consider that:

- We already know this—we're simply remembering.
- We're only seeing what already is, but is being overlooked.
- We don't need to have any theoretical knowledge, special words, or background.
- We don't need teachers or authorities in order to discover this.
- We don't need to believe; we can find our own proof.

Essential to inquiry is the Zen concept of *Beginner's Mind*:

- Look in this moment with *fresh eyes* as a small child would.
- Forget all knowledge and past experience.
- Leave all beliefs behind, including all spiritual beliefs and anything you've ever read or heard about awakening.
- Let go of all expectations, ideas, and goals.

Don't bring anything to the inquiry except naked attention. Put away your spiritual ideas, including the books and videos they come from. Let inquiry pull you into itself. Keep it very, very simple. Keep it so simple that the mind has nothing to do and lets go of trying to understand or manipulate. That is when real inquiry can happen.

To support this approach, I've kept the book's text as lean as possible. Every word counts. Don't rush through it, but savor the text (especially the inquiries) in small bites. Everything nonessential has been removed. Repetition is used as a tool to help erode beliefs. The result is that this is not an entertaining book. It's a workbook.

No Teachers

What nondual inquiry points to must be recognized from direct observation, or it will remain a well-written menu that never produces the taste of the meal. Once the understanding is reawakened and alive, inquiry is no longer needed. See the last chapter for more about being done.

Nonduality is not a teaching. The concept of *teaching* assumes a teacher, students, and knowledge gained through the teaching. But nonduality is just a communication of our natural state. It only requires removing existing knowledge to see it clearly.

Teaching nonduality would be like teaching someone how to breathe air or drink water. There's nothing wrong with it. It may be interesting. It may be a helpful reminder. But we don't need it. You don't need me or anyone else to teach you anything. There is no teaching in this book.

What you *need* is already within you, and inquiry is pointing you to that recognition. This removes the stress over teachers, teachings, and paths. There's nothing to be taught—just noticing or re-cognizing what is already the case. The only thing to *do* is investigate the beliefs and assumptions currently blocking the noticing. Only you can do this. It's done through inquiry. You are your own teacher.

If there's nothing to get, there's also nothing to expect. Although it seems impossible, try to let go of any expectations about what is supposed to happen, especially when and how insights will occur. No one knows how this will unfold through your unique bodymind. It will take however long it takes. These are sobering messages. But try to remember why you are doing this, and take only that honest intention to awaken into the inquiry. Nothing more.

A Noticing

An inquiry is meant to show you something. Then it can be discarded. It is not meant to convince you of anything. Only you know whether the inquiry has done its job. If it produces no a-ha moment or insight after several days, move on to the next inquiry and return to this one later.

We're not trying to get rid of anything or add anything new. And we're not trying to remove the self! The self sticks around and continues its selfing, but is no longer taken so seriously. What we've seen through the inquiries still appears, but becomes insubstantial and no longer hooks us.

We're not trying to create an experience of expansion or deeper awareness. There's no such thing. We're not trying to become *more* aware, either. We can't become more of what we already are. The inquiries will show you this, so don't worry if it sounds confusing now.

This is only about seeing and noticing. It's never about a new or different experience, because experiences come and go—no matter how joyful, horrible, or expansive. This is about what is permanent.

Nondual awareness is not a deeper or greater experience that happens to a separate self, but rather a recognition of Awareness as all there ever is. It's realizing we already *are* this aware Presence and are already experiencing that *all the time*.

Reality feels like a separate, personal experience because that's how we interpret it. Occasionally, the self may even feel it's having a peak awareness experience (in deep meditation, for example). But that's not it! Experiences come and go. Awareness is realized to be true no matter what the experience.

Beyond Appearances

When we start the process of inquiry, we usually believe Awareness refers to *my* awareness. It feels like the light gray dot in the figures below: within the mind, likely in the brain. Awareness seems to refer to *my conscious attention.* We start to inquire and seem to experience states of more or less awareness. These states come and go. But we're still looking from within the mind and believing Awareness to be something we get to instead of noticing that it is *always already there.*

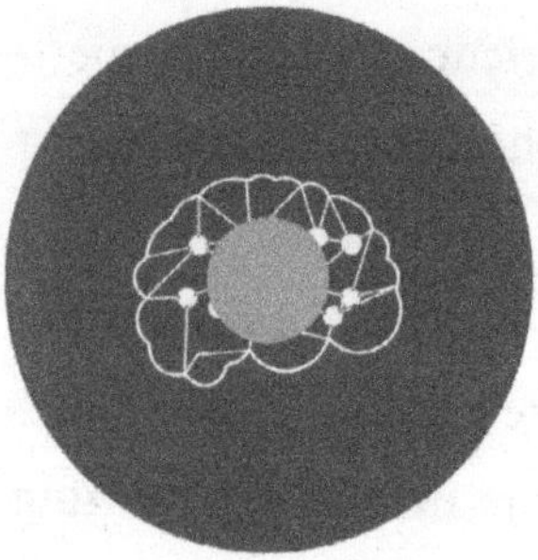

BODY-MIND

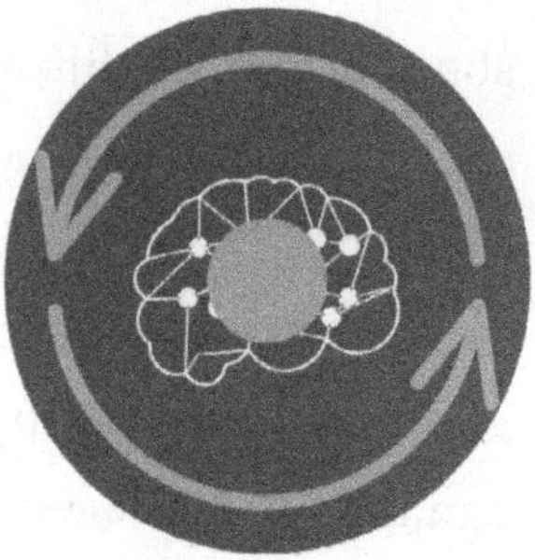

BODY-MIND

At first, we are convinced that Awareness is personal, existing inside our minds. Later we realize that Awareness is aware of the mind and seems to surround it.

In inquiry, we begin to notice that what is aware is always *aware of* thought and perception—which is all the body-mind ever consists of. We're already aware of the body-mind and can't be contained by it. Now it can feel like we're observing life from *above and behind* the body. This still seems like we're paying conscious attention or like a state that comes and goes. It still feels personal, and we still experience ourselves as separate.

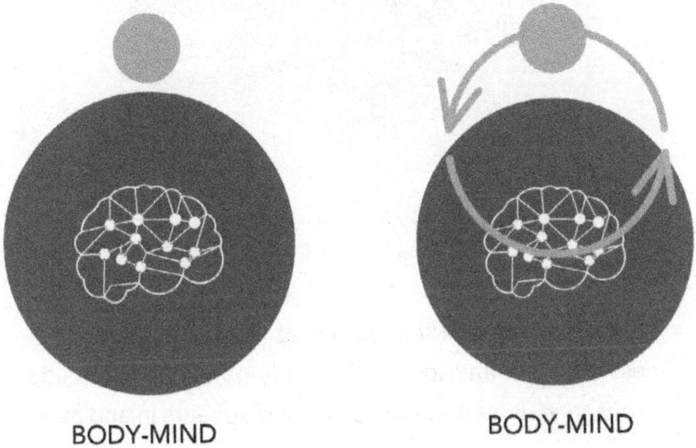

Next, we realize that Awareness is aware of the body-mind, so it can't be locked within it. The observer perspective can seem to come and go, expanding and contracting back into the body-mind.

At some point, we realize Awareness is always already there. It is more fundamental and constant than the body or mind. We discover we *are* this ordinary, aware Presence. It's not personal, not *my limited awareness,* but infinitely more. The body-mind appears *in/as* Awareness, not the other way around.

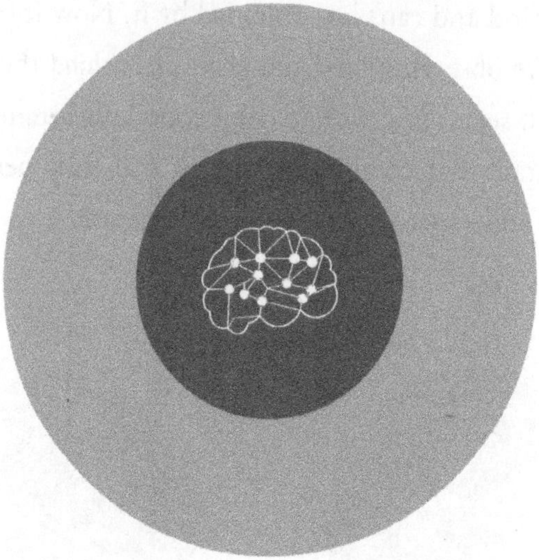

Here a fundamental shift occurs, as we realize that Awareness is neither an aspect of the body-mind nor an outside observer. It is what the body-mind appears in and as.

Eventually, we realize Awareness is all there ever is. We can't be limited to a body or mind. Those are spontaneous appearances that come and go in our aware Being. We stop identifying with the body-mind. We realize Awareness is unitive, one. And we see that there is no separate self: the edges of both circles in the image dissolve. Everything is one field. Please keep in mind that these are attempts to describe something that is essentially indescribable. We're attempting to visualize the type of shift that occurs with inquiry.

A Shift in Identification

The only thing that actually *occurs* is a shift of identification. Instead of identifying with a limited, separate self in a vast, cold universe, I discover that I am already this universal Presence itself.

Don't Believe Anything

Inquiry is never asking us to believe in anything, and that includes any nondual principles. It's not trying to prove anything either. It's only an attempt to cast reasonable doubt on the assumption that you are a separate self. Reasonable doubt is more than enough!

What we discover in the inquiries erodes our core belief that there is a self and that we are this self. We look at the self from different angles and remove all the layers of what it could be. What is left is what **You** already are (and already were) but weren't noticing.

As soon as we see a belief to be false upon investigation, it can never hook us again. The thought may continue to appear, and we may even give attention to it for a while, but the unquestioned belief in it is gone for good.

Identifying as a Separate Self	Identifying as Aware Presence
I am this body-mind. It's my job to control and develop it.	The body-mind is real but also an appearance in what I am.
I am defined by my story, my narrative of myself.	The narrative is irrelevant as it's not about what I am.
I believe I'm the doer of my life, with free will and volition.	Life happens spontaneously; there's nothing to manage or control.
I must work to define, protect, and promote myself. I compete.	I'm not interested in defining, protecting, or promoting a self.
I'm a small, vulnerable self in a vast, physical world.	*This* is one, indivisible—everything all at once.
I need goals and purpose in life; life must have meaning.	Life, pure existence, is more than I will ever need.
My self is never done, never good enough or whole.	Wholeness is all there is. It's already complete.
I am on a linear path from past to future. I have to achieve something.	There is only the eternal *now* and nothing to achieve. Being is everything.

For many, these beliefs stop appearing altogether. But since we don't control how this happens, we don't need to worry about when or how this occurs! Don't try to be clever in inquiry. This isn't a debate to win or an intelligence test to ace. That is more of an intellectual exercise than an inquiry. Do bring your skepticism, but be willing to let go of all you know.

Finally, don't believe anything in this book, either! Find out for yourself what is true. Once again this means you don't need a teacher, a guru, or a guide beyond some simple, essential inquiry instructions. The point is to find out on your own.

However, if you get unbearably stuck, it's a good idea to find a guide to get you unstuck. As mentioned before, finding a guide has become much easier with the advent of the internet. You can find some additional resources at the end of this book.

A nondual understanding comes from the direct recognition of it, nothing else.

That direct recognition comes through inquiry.

Not from feeling something in particular.

Not from experiencing a state.

And definitely not from thinking.

How to Inquire

Don't just read the menu. You have to taste the meal.

Where You Should Be Looking . . .

Inquiry points you back to the container of all experience, again and again and again, until it is clear that **You** are the container and not the contents.

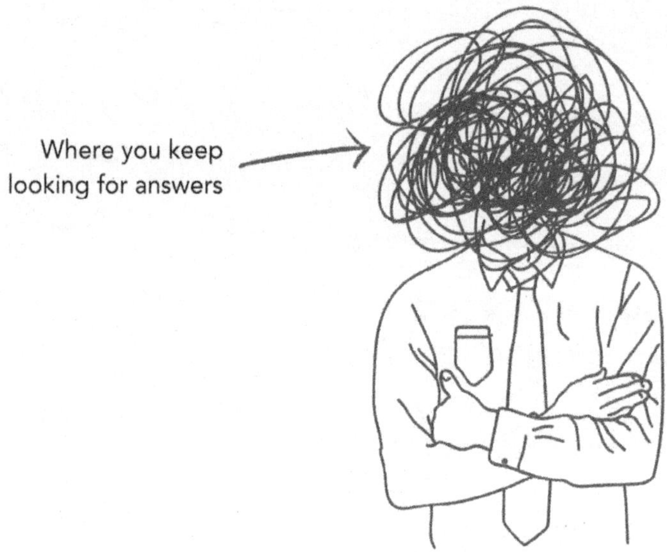

Accept the Paradox

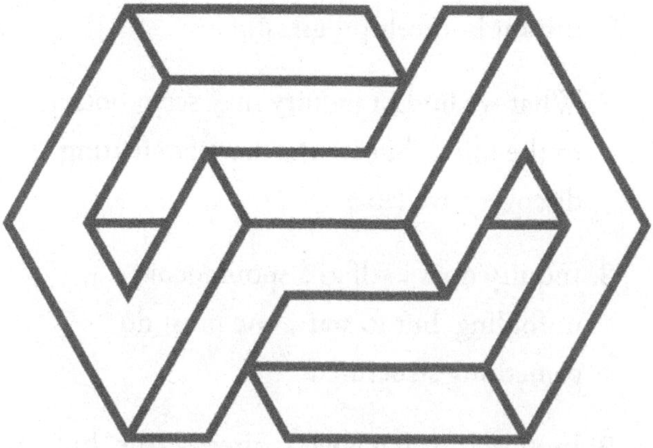

1. Inquiry is not a practice, but paradoxically, it must be practiced in order to discover this.
2. Sometimes an inquiry seems like it's a mindfulness meditation, but it never is: It's noticing what is aware of being mindful.
3. Inquiry is unfocusing attention from the content of experience, but it takes focused attention to do so.
4. Inquiry is not thinking, but it requires thinking to process what we have seen directly.
5. Inquiry is wordless, but to explain it we need language.

6. There is no improving or deepening inquiry. It's complete from the very first instant but feels progressive.

7. What we find in inquiry may seem boring to the mind, but it's the most fascinating discovery available.

8. Inquiry does itself as a spontaneous unfolding, but to start, one must do something structured.

9. Inquiry is seeing what is already true, but at first we can't see that. It feels like we're looking for something that is not currently available.

10. Inquiry points to what is beyond the mind, but whatever we see is also always and immediately filtered through the mind.

Realizing What We're Not: The Via Negativa

The diagram on the next page illustrates the negative way of inquiry. Like peeling layers off an onion, we peel away the illusory self—each level represented in the graphic—by inquiring at each layer of the onion. At each level, we inquire: *Am I this?*

WHAT WE'RE NOT
THOUGHTS
BELIEFS
OUR STORY
SENSATIONS
PERCEPTIONS
A BODY
THE AUTHOR
OR DOER
SEPARATE
me
THE SENSE OF
BEING A SELF
LOCATED IN
SPACE / TIME
WHAT WE ARE
ALIVE
AWARE, PRESENT
INFINITE, ETERNAL
ONE

Right now, **You** are not a separate self. But because almost all of us are completely identified with that illusion, we must dedicate much inquiry to seeing through the various layers of this concept.

The negative way is about subtraction. When we see through everything we're not, what we're left with is nothing. But we don't disappear! We're still here—an alive and aware Presence that is undeniable and inescapable.

Realizing What We Are: The Via Contemplativa

What we are is depicted by the chart's inner circle. **You** are all of it. **You** are the entire Universe. In the Awareness Inquiries in this book, we discover that **You** are all there ever is, was, or will be.

Remember that giving what we are any name at all makes it seem like an object or thing apart from us. What we are is not a thing, has no content, and can't be experienced. Whether we call it Awareness or Presence, Being or Knowing, Consciousness or Source, no name adequately expresses it.

So, the pathless path described in this book is meant to help us realize what we're not and rediscover what we are. That's all there is to it: to see both of these clearly, beyond doubt.

Seeing All Sides

Inquiry can only be complete if it helps us see both sides of the truth: what we're not (a self) and what we are (our true nature). Talking about two sides of the truth is a construct to help us make sense of this: there aren't really any sides to the truth. Nondual traditions tend to focus on either one or the other: what we are or what we aren't. It's hard to find a form of inquiry that looks at them both. The spiral graphic below illustrates that inquiry is ideally a dance between the two and a continuum of both.

Here we see that one axis shows that we are self and no self, while the other axis shows that inquiry is both a practice and not a practice. At first, it feels like inquiry is practice that the self engages in at specific times in order to achieve a goal, even if the goal is just insight. However, we eventually see that inquiry is not a practice but something spontaneous. Inquiry does us. It gradually becomes clear that inquiry isn't separate from life: Inquiry is living this life while knowing/being our true nature.

The Practice That Is No Practice

Inquiry feels like a practice until it goes beyond the mind. As mentioned before, it becomes clear later that it happens spontaneously. It gradually becomes obvious that we are only recognizing what is already the case beyond the mind, and that there is no inquirer to make inquiry happen.

American nonduality teacher John Wheeler had this to say about self-inquiry:

> *It is tempting to try to turn self-inquiry into a technique or practice. Then you are off to the races again as a person who is now doing self-inquiry and (hopefully) getting closer and closer to something (yourself, I presume!). To me, self-inquiry is just looking to see if*

the imagined separate entity at the root of all seeking is really present.

Inquiry is noticing reality without our belief filters. When we start out doing that, it's helpful to have specific instructions. That's why this book contains thirty-three inquiries presented in a specific order. They begin as more general questions, followed by further comments and observations, and then more detailed questions that dig deeper. But although they are presented as questions, remember that we're not asking our minds to come up with an answer. We don't want to think about them at all if we can help it, although that's easier said than done.

The questions are investigations to contemplate. Take one on and let it percolate in the background throughout the day. You don't have to set aside half an hour to focus on it, although you can do so if this method appeals to you.

You may experience strong resistance to inquiry at first, and at various points beyond that. This resistance is a good sign! It means there is a pull towards rediscovering things the little self doesn't want to look at. Don't fight or try to break through resistance. Accept it and let it play out. This process does itself.

The Layers of the Onion

The inquiries are presented in a tested and recommended order. Inquiries later in the book make more sense when we have already seen through the initial layers of the self. Because we are so identified with the body-mind, most of us need to carefully see what we are not before we can truly rediscover what we are.

The idea is to complete the inquiries in the given order as they move from what we are not to focus solely on what we are. I recommend that you do no more than one inquiry a day. You might even stay with one inquiry for days or weeks before moving on. I further recommend doing some inquiry daily and not letting too much time pass between contemplations. This keeps the momentum of seeing going. Since there's no one in control of this process, I'm just planting some ideas for those readers who believe they need structure. It's really out of our hands.

Inquiry can also be entirely spontaneous; it may play out this way for you. Browse through the book and try an inquiry that speaks to you. If it doesn't seem to open up anything right now, try a different one. Follow your intuition, because although there is a recommended progression, that doesn't necessarily mean that it will be the right order of inquiries for you. Everyone is a unique unfolding. Just remember that it's best to engage with all the inquiries at some point.

You may find it helpful to write down the observations from your inquiry. Yes, writing requires thinking. In order to write your insights down, those insights need to be processed through the mind, but the mind is always processing anyway. Writing can help you internalize what you have seen, though I recommend limiting your writing to simply making a few notes, rather than treating it as a journaling exercise. Brief notes can help you see what clarity there is when reviewed later. But don't view these notes as truth to hang on to. Nothing seen in the past is of any use *now*.

Fear and Resistance

For many of us, inquiry will bring up some fear. This feeling will likely be brief. It will be easy to observe and ignore during inquiry. For some, fear can be more like a dark night of the soul, where it feels as though we'll be swallowed up into a black hole of despair. There's no way to predict what it will be like for you.

Is fear, along with the resistance that comes up as an attempt to avoid fear, a sign of a self refusing to die? Perhaps. But that would be yet another belief about a series of continually changing sensations. It would be giving what we call fear far too much power.

Resistance can take many forms. It can show up as unbearable boredom, or as suddenly finding other more important things to do. It can show up as questioning our sanity for even considering inquiring. Or it could simply mean not inquiring.

Resistance and the sensations we call fear are normal reactions to questioning the self. However, in essence, even the strongest fear is never more than a set of sensations coming and going in what we are. They don't mean anything until the mind comes in with beliefs and interpretations.

There is no advice for dealing with fear or resistance. These feelings will play themselves out. They will stop you from inquiring or they won't. They will occur and stick around for however long they do. Try not to worry about it. Don't make it into anything bigger than it is, although even that is not under your control.

The fact that you're reading this means that this process is already doing you. Fear and resistance may be an inevitable part of that, or there may be no fear at all. Remember that an emotion can't do anything. Sensations have no inherent power except for the power you give them through belief. This too shall pass.

All or Nothing

It can be useful to know about two common problems that come up during inquiry. Awareness of them can help us identify the situation when it occurs and ensure we don't stay stuck there.

The first problem is when we understand no-self conceptually and try to *make ourselves believe* in no-self. We try to believe we don't exist. This quickly deteriorates into: "There's nothing to do, and it's all pointless, so why am I even alive?" Some turn away from nonduality and inquiry here, believing it to be nihilism.

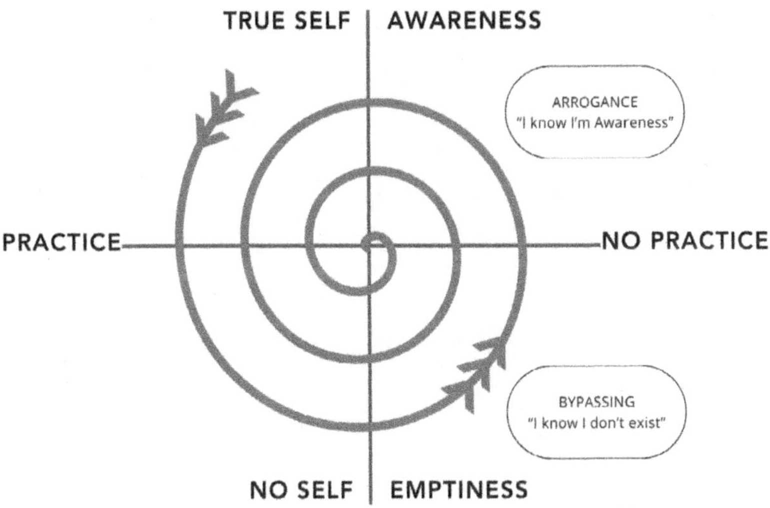

The remedy is to see clearly what we are: the Awareness side of the spiral. We are not nothing, we are everything! But we can get stuck here as well, in the spiritual ego. Now we try to make ourselves believe that we're all-encompassing Awareness! However, this is still a self. The difference is that now it's trying to believe it is God. The remedy lies on the opposite side of the spiral—seeing clearly that there is no self! It's crucial to see both sides of the equation.

One apparent day in Eternity,

A tiny part of an Infinite Ocean briefly forgot what it was and mistakenly came to believe it was limited to Dave the Wave.

For many apparent years, Dave struggled.

Dave struggled to wave, to improve,
and to be the best wave ever.

Dave suffered under comparison with other waves, had fears about the end of wave life, and felt scared and alone.

One day, the Ocean in the form of
Dave rediscovered it was Ocean.

And the idea of Dave ended.

The Eternal Ocean remained.

Part II

33 Essential Inquiries

About the Inquiries

The inquiries in this book are adapted from various sources. All spiritual lineages and wisdom traditions have taught some form of inquiry. Countless nonduality teachers teach their unique versions. Many have influenced the inquiries presented here.

There are many more possible inquiries than the ones in this book, of course. I have only included the ones I consider to be essential, because they are the inquiries that will lead to understanding.

The core inquiries are about what we are, our true nature. These inquiries are sprinkled throughout, but become the sole focus toward the end. These Awareness Inquiries are always pointing to what is already the case. But first, we must peel back the six layers of what we are not, so this is where we start.

You will notice many questions and considerations are repetitive. This is by design, and is because we're looking at the same truth from all possible angles. If something is unclear from an earlier inquiry, a different example, a new phrase, or a new point in the process can call forth that clarity.

The inquiries progress from the top to the bottom of the image on the next page and are marked with their corresponding icon. Ultimately, though, we are always exploring the same eternal truth.

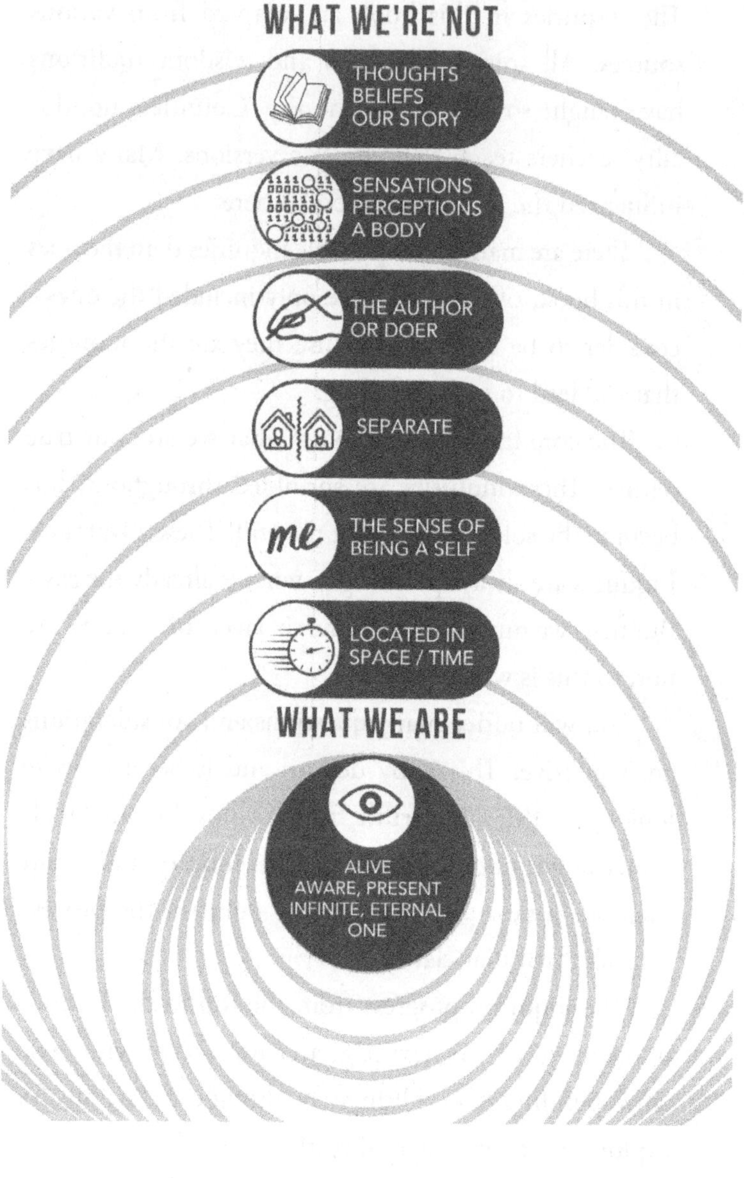
WHAT WE'RE NOT
THOUGHTS
BELIEFS
OUR STORY
SENSATIONS
PERCEPTIONS
A BODY
THE AUTHOR
OR DOER
SEPARATE
me
THE SENSE OF
BEING A SELF
LOCATED IN
SPACE / TIME
WHAT WE ARE
ALIVE
AWARE, PRESENT
INFINITE, ETERNAL
ONE

What is *I* or *me*? How would you describe yourself?

- What are you referring to when you say *I* or *me*?
- Imagine that you're trying to explain what a human being is to an alien who magically speaks your language.
    - ▹ What words would you use?
    - ▹ Describe this as clearly as you can.
- You might consider the following:
    - ▹ Are you your body?
    - ▹ Are you your mind or brain?
    - ▹ Are you your character or personality?
- This is not an intelligence test! Don't try to find the supposedly correct nondual answer. Don't answer what you think you should. Write down your honest thoughts about what you currently believe to be true. Then put your notes away and forget about them. We will return to this question at the end of the book.

THOUGHTS
BELIEFS
OUR STORY

Can *You* have any problems if there are no thoughts?

- Notice that for there to be a problem, there must be thoughts about a problem.
- Explore whether this is true by looking at some examples from your life. Think about this question using bigger and smaller problems.
- **Is it possible to have a problem without thinking?**
- What does this tell us about the cause of problems?
- Does what is *aware of* thinking ever have a problem?
- Does the living Presence reading these words right now have problems?
- **Look carefully at what is, and notice:**
    - ▹ The obsession with thoughts.
    - ▹ How we give them importance and value.
    - ▹ That there's no need to do anything beyond noticing.
- See how we've learned to immediately and unconditionally give all our attention to our thinking?
- See how we simply *assume* that thoughts are credible because they say something about the person we believe we are?

- Notice that this also applies to thinking about or attempting to understand nonduality.
- There is nothing wrong and nothing you don't know or understand if you don't think about it.
- There is no issue with anything that happens or doesn't happen. There is no problem with any kind of experience or lack of experience.
- Only thought says "I'm not getting it," "This can't be it," or "I'm not resting in Awareness enough."
- **Where are you when you're not thinking?**

AWARENESS

Are *You* alive? Are *You* experiencing life?

- **Are You alive?** This is a simple, obvious question, but crucial to examine before continuing. You may nod and say, "Yes, this is obvious, now let's get to the juicy stuff!" Resist that urge and stay with this question until there is a shift.

- **You must be alive to experience anything at all.**

- Even if you answer *I don't know* to the original question, you must be alive to say so.

    - ▹ Alive Presence is always already there—if it wasn't, there would be nothing to experience.

    - ▹ It doesn't matter what the experience is. It could be complete absorption in thoughts or feelings, but even that experience is still being experienced.

- **If there were no Awareness, you would be dead.** Consider whether this is true.

- Notice that you don't *do* Aliveness. It just is, spontaneously.

    - ▹ **You can't make it happen or go away.**

    - ▹ Notice that Aliveness is completely natural and effortless.

- ▹ Notice again that this aware Presence is always already there. It's the only aspect of experience that is never absent!
- ▹ **You already are Aliveness.**

- **This alive Presence is your essential nature, right *now*.**
    - ▹ This Awareness is ordinary, nothing special. We are not talking about a special experience or a deeper state.
    - ▹ We're only noticing what already is and what is already given, no matter what state the body-mind is in or what feelings and experiences it is having.
    - ▹ **It is right there even when you believe it isn't.**
- If you fully realized that **You** are this Aliveness right now, the search would be over and there would be no need for the rest of this book.

AWARENESS

What is aware of reading these words?

- **What, right now, is Aware of reading this?**
    - ▹ Don't think, but notice that attention goes somewhere to answer. Then notice what that *somewhere* is.
    - ▹ Notice the open space this question points out, often felt as a spaciousness behind the head at first.
    - ▹ Nothing is supposed to happen. It's just noticing what's already there, like the wide-open sky around the clouds or the white of the page around these words.
    - ▹ This can feel empty, uninteresting, or even boring to the mind. Try to ignore those feelings and investigate anyway.
    - ▹ During the day, ask this question when it spontaneously occurs. Relax and briefly notice what is already Aware.
- **What is Aware of seeing/hearing/sensing?**
    - ▹ Notice the aware space already there in the background.
    - ▹ All we're doing is looking. Just a simple, direct look at what we already are but weren't seeing.

- This is not a practice; there's no effort involved. It's a noticing, like noticing the screen while watching a movie.

    - ▹ Right now, notice what is already Aware of everything. Let it happen, and don't force it. Look again, however briefly, at what is always already there and Aware.

    - ▹ Putting attention or focus on Awareness **isn't necessary for it to exist.** There is always Awareness already. If there were not, there would be no experience.

- **There is a difference between attention (focus) and Awareness itself.** There is always an aware Presence in the background. But that doesn't mean we're always aware *of* it.

    - ▹ It's not necessary or possible to always be aware of Awareness. That would give you a monster headache!

    - ▹ It doesn't matter if there is no awareness of Awareness for long stretches. Remaining aware of Awareness is not a goal.

THOUGHTS
BELIEFS
OUR STORY

Where does a thought come from? Where does it go?

- **Can you notice where thoughts appear from?**
- **Can you see where a thought goes when it disappears?**
- Thoughts are vibrations, mental energy. We can imagine the mind or brain as a radio that tunes in and picks up some of these vibrations.
    - ▹ **Do you make these mental vibrations happen or do they just appear and disappear?**
    - ▹ Doesn't it seem likely that vibrations simply arise and you pick up on them, allowing them to move through you and then disappear from the mind?
- We can also imagine the mind (or brain) as a sixth sense organ. It senses thoughts as the eyes sense light.
- Thinking is a natural process. **But does thinking require a thinker?**
- Investigate: **Can a thought *do* anything?**
    - ▹ Does it have any power in and of itself?
    - ▹ Or is a thought just mental energy?

- ▹ If you think the thought *pink elephant*, does a pink elephant now exist?
- ▹ Do any thoughts create reality? Look carefully at this one, because we are constantly told that they do.

- **Is it necessary to believe thoughts?**
    - ▹ Look at some thoughts you believe are true. **Do you have to believe them?** Does anything change about reality if you don't believe them?
    - ▹ What is the difference between a thought and a belief?
    - ▹ Isn't a belief simply a thought that is believed?

THOUGHTS
BELIEFS
OUR STORY

How do you know thoughts or emotions are yours?

- **Are any of your thoughts truly original?** Things you've never heard or read anywhere before?
- **Do you choose thoughts?**
    - Can you choose to have different thoughts?
    - If so, then why would you ever think negative thoughts?
    - The mind is an endless thought stream.
    - Thoughts, when we believe them, can cause feelings which then lead to more thoughts.
- **You are aware of the mind, so how can you be it?**
    - It appears to **You**, so it can't be what **You** are.
    - You say *my* mind, *my* feelings, and *my* thoughts.
    - **How do you know that they are yours?**
    - Why is a thought that appears *your* thought? You didn't create it. You can't make it happen or not happen.
    - The brain is the sense organ that perceives thoughts, exactly as the ear perceives sounds. It's not your sound that the ear

hears or your thought that the brain perceives.

- **What about feelings?** Do you choose what you feel?
    - ▹ Look carefully at your raw experience. We have many beliefs about feelings and emotions.
    - ▹ **Are you doing the feeling?** Or does it just come and go?
- **If thoughts are impersonal, so are emotions.**
    - ▹ Emotions are a mixture of thoughts and sensations we've learned to give names, such as fear. They can stick around longer than thoughts, but they still come and go spontaneously.
    - ▹ You're not creating the feeling. And what **You** are is not touched by the emotion. **You** are aware *of* the emotion.
- Thoughts and feelings are just one aspect of what is going on in Aliveness. They're spontaneous and conditioned.
- If no value is given to the sensations and they're given no attention or meaning, there is no resistance or suffering.

THOUGHTS
BELIEFS
OUR STORY

Who are *You* without your story?

- **Can you describe who you are without telling a story about yourself?** It's impossible.
  - ▹ Notice how this story, this narrative, has changed over time.
  - ▹ **How can it be true if it changes, often drastically?**
- What beliefs about yourself have changed or disappeared altogether?
  - ▹ If you have siblings or can ask your parents, compare notes on what happened to you as you were growing up. Do the narratives match?
  - ▹ Notice how you tell different stories about yourself depending on the context and the audience.
- Look at some roles you identify with strongly: parent, coach, expert, friend. Feel yourself in each role, with all the behavior that entails, including the emotions and stories that come with it.
  - ▹ **Where is this identity when you're not in that role?**
  - ▹ **You** are not this behavior or narrative. It's what the body thinks and does at certain times, but it is not what you always are.

    - ▹ Roles are concepts and ideas we add to reality. We are not our behavior or the story about it. **You** are the theater in which the play is staged, not the character in the play.

- **Does telling a story about a *me* make it real?**
    - ▹ If I tell a story about Sherlock Holmes, does that make him real?
    - ▹ Are you real because you tell a story about yourself and then believe it? We're not referring to the body, only to the story.
    - ▹ Look at your complete self-narrative, the story of *me*. Take in your complete past, all your memories, everything you have ever experienced. This is your identity. It is a fabrication. **It is not You. It is a story about you.**
    - ▹ Belief in this story creates a prison of identity. Your story is a made-up world of beliefs. If you see that it's not real and you no longer believe it, it can't cause suffering.

- **You** (Awareness) have no story. **You** (Aliveness) are free.

THOUGHTS
BELIEFS
OUR STORY

What is your mind? Is there anything to call *my mind*?

- **Can you find something called *my mind*?**
    - ▹ Can you find anything substantial beyond a never-ending stream of thoughts and sensations that we interpret as a specific feeling or emotion?
    - ▹ **Is there such a thing as a personal mind?**
    - ▹ **How do you know?**
- The personal, private mind is a concept. We believe it is housed in the brain. Is it?
    - ▹ How would you know that from direct experience?
    - ▹ Can you find anything we could call the mind beyond thoughts and sensations?
- The brain behaves like a hard drive of some sort. It stores information, thoughts, and memories, but not without distortion. Then it replays this information filtered through further beliefs, biases, and assumptions.
- The brain may be like a thought receiver, much like a radio receives radio waves. These vibrations are translated into language and thoughts.
- Neither analogy makes it *my* mind.

- **The obsession with *my psychology* is powerful.**
    - ▹ We've been conditioned for decades to put all our attention, value, and belief on the supposed mind and its contents.
    - ▹ We have learned many popular theories about the mind, including such concepts as the subconscious, the reptilian brain, and left- and right-brain thinking. But these are not known in direct experience. They are theories.
    - ▹ This is deep conditioning. Don't expect these ideas to disappear. But we can start to see they are only *ideas.*

AWARENESS

What has always been here, experiencing life?

- Don't try to answer, but notice where the question points: **What has always been here, experiencing life?**
  - ▹ What was here when you were five years old, fifteen years old, and is still here today? What will be here when you are eighty?
  - ▹ It is always the same aware Aliveness. It doesn't come or go.
  - ▹ **Your essential Being is always the same. It is eternal.**
- Take a metaphorical step *back* from the mind. This pulls us into what seems like the background.
  - ▹ It can seem like a spacious, silent vastness, or a vibrating, energetic field of potential. It doesn't feel personal at all.
  - ▹ There is no knowledge and there are no concepts here. There is only Aliveness, Being, knowing life as it is now.
- **Silently and effortlessly look at this Being,** this aware Presence. The verb *looking* is used as shorthand for perception. We are not trying to see anything.
  - ▹ Don't worry about anything happening or doing this right. **Just try to look.** Look

directly at this alive, aware sense of Being without trying to perceive or understand anything.

  - ▹ It doesn't matter how long you look. A fraction of a second is enough. Try, with all your heart, to notice and recognize what is aware.

- Notice that this aware Presence isn't empty or a void. It is vibrantly conscious and aware. The mind can't understand this. It doesn't compute mentally. So, to the mind, this Presence can feel boring or scary: an empty infinite hole or void that will swallow us up. If such thoughts or feelings come up, just notice them and let them pass.

- Presence is sometimes described as a warm, subtly tingling Aliveness. But don't worry if it doesn't feel that way for you. This Awareness is the very presence of **You**.

- **You** have never been born. **You** will never die.

You Are Not Your Thoughts

Consider that thinking may be occurring completely in parallel to life. Perhaps thinking is nothing more than the mental chatter we add to reality. Before you learned a language as a small child, there was no thinking and life still happened just fine.

Whether there is thinking or not does not influence reality. Could that be true? Then what is the point of quieting or emptying the mind? We can simply let thinking be and pay it no attention.

There is nothing wrong with thinking per se. If there's a long stretch of thinking, that is just what is occurring. It's neither good nor bad unless we believe it is. Thinking is the result of automatic programming running on the hardware of the body.

Thinking is not completely useless, of course. Useful thinking may happen spontaneously and appropriately—for example, as a tool to communicate with others. But thinking about an imaginary separate self is rarely necessary.

Consider that the self itself is nothing more than a thought, the I-thought. This thought isn't controlled by any separate entity. The self-thought arises and disappears spontaneously like any other thought. **If we're not thinking me-thoughts, there is no me!**

Remember that a thought can't do anything; it has no power or agency. Therefore, this self we believe in so strongly is nothing more than a mental vibration without agency or volition. It's only a repetitive thought pattern. **The self is a mental loop in love with itself, selfing automatically on endless repeat.**

We only feel the *me* is robust and important because we have been taught to give it all our attention. Me-thoughts make us feel individual and special. No-self is not a popular proposition to the selfing loop!

What It's Like to See This

The quest for a better *me* never ends. All day long the thoughts come: "Am I doing enough? Is what I'm doing good enough? Am I growing, learning, succeeding?"

There's often a strong belief that when we have realized enough, thoughts will quiet down or disappear altogether, especially the negative ones. We will overcome overthinking and certainly any negative thinking. This is just more of the self's self-improvement spiel. Thinking is not being done by anyone. Thoughts appear and disappear to no one.

This is the only thing that changed upon seeing this: There is no longer belief in an entity called *me* that can take ownership of thoughts. Self-referencing thoughts are always untrue because they refer to no one.

Where before a thought about me was breaking news, it is now irrelevant. And yes, for whatever reason they're also vastly reduced in number.

There is no longer any sense of lack or defectiveness. There is a knowing that everything and everyone is already complete and free, so there is nothing to do, improve, or seek. There is no belief going into the thoughts, meaning there is no psychological suffering, stress, or worry. Sometimes belief does go into a thought for a while and there is worry or tension. Then it is seen through or the thought disappears. Without belief in the I-thought this doesn't matter, as it is happening to no one.

There is a beautiful freedom in not needing to have an identity and not needing to be anyone. There is no constriction around a story or set of beliefs. My story is irrelevant. If someone attacks the supposed story of me, that is not a problem anymore. Who cares what so-called others think of my so-called story?

SENSATIONS
PERCEPTIONS
A BODY

If you are in a body, why don't you experience that?

- **Why don't we experience the body from inside it? If we're (in) the body, shouldn't we experience that in some sense?**
    - ▹ Close your eyes and try to experience the body as a whole. Is that possible?
    - ▹ We experience an endless stream of sensations that come and go. Do you make any of these appear? Or do they spontaneously appear and disappear?
    - ▹ All we experience is a tingling here, a burning there. These sensations come and go.
    - ▹ We've learned to think that these sensations are occurring inside our bodies. **But there is no direct experience of that.**
    - ▹ Scan upward through what you think is the body, beginning at your toes. **Can you find where you are located inside it?**
    - ▹ Does the fact of having sensations prove that there is a body?
- If you forget everything you know, what remains? Just some sensory perceptions, sensations, shapes, and colors?

- **Does the appearance of a set of changing sensations that we call a body mean that you are in there?**
- **How would you prove you are in the body?**
    - ▹ Look at your hand. Does it seem realistic that you are inside the hand? Does it seem realistic for any other body part?
    - ▹ What about the head? If you forget what you've learned, **does it seem likely from direct observation that you're in your head?**
    - ▹ If we put you in a sensory deprivation tank and shut down your brain, do you still exist?
    - ▹ Do you exist in deep sleep when there are no sensory perceptions or experiences from the body? Or do you stop existing for a few hours every night?

SENSATIONS
PERCEPTIONS
A BODY

Look in the mirror—is that you in there?

- Take your time with this inquiry and don't listen to any derisive thoughts—just do it! Go to a mirror now and actually look at your reflection.
    - ▹ **If the image that appears in the mirror is you, then what is it that is observing the image in the mirror?**
    - ▹ Is the image in the mirror also you? Are you in two different places?
    - ▹ Now close your eyes and bring your attention to the head, where most people feel they are located.
    - ▹ **Are you inside the head?**
    - ▹ Is the self somewhere behind the forehead?
    - ▹ It only feels that way because the visual sense is strongest for most of us. **There is no direct evidence** that we are in the head or behind the forehead.
    - ▹ Step away from the mirror and once again contemplate everything you call *my body* all at once.

- ▹ If you lose body parts, do you still exist? How many body parts can one lose before the *me* stops existing?
- ▹ **How do you know?**

- Over the course of your life, almost all the cells in the body have been renewed. Most of the body is new compared to a few years or decades ago. Can you then be the body?
- A baby has no sense of a body. They have to learn what is part of their body and what isn't. This takes much repetition.
- Many times during the day, we have no awareness of the body at all. We even need practices such as yoga or bodywork to become aware of the body!
- On direct evidence, **there is no body to be found and no *me or self* to be found inside it.**

SENSATIONS
PERCEPTIONS
A BODY

Can you find an edge to the body?

- **Where does your body end and the rest of the world begin?**

    - ▹ Can you find the edge of the body, its exact location? Don't just mentally say, "Yes, of course I can," but investigate in direct experience.

    - ▹ Close your eyes and try to find this edge now before reading further. Scan through what seems like the body and try to find the specific point or location where it ends and the rest of the world begins.

    - ▹ Open your eyes and see what we call skin. The mind tells you that this is the border because that is what we learned.

    - ▹ But if you ignore that, the visual impression of what we call *skin* is nothing more than a visual perception. We need to mentally add the ideas of body, skin, and border.

    - ▹ **Can you determine that sensations are coming from inside the body?** How can you do this if there is no border?

    - ▹ Notice that sensations simply arise in Awareness. You must add thinking (using your mind) to locate those sensations inside the mental concept of *body.*

- ▹ **You have to use the mind to construct the idea of a body.**
- ▹ None of the sensations *come with the information* that they are inside a body.

• **What about feeling your body and not another's body?** Notice that *my body* and *your body* are further mental constructs. The mind adds these concepts to reality.

- ▹ Sensations arise and disappear, and then the mind adds the idea that they are in *my body*, which must be why I feel them. Or they are in *your body*, which is why I don't feel them.
- ▹ But everything—all bodies and all sensations—is just appearances in Awareness. See how *we* add the concepts of you and me to the raw sensory data.

SENSATIONS
PERCEPTIONS
A BODY

If pain occurs, does what is aware of the pain suffer?

- **The body is the experiencing organism, so experience will always seem local and separate.**
    - ▹ The body transmits experiences through the sense organs. These experiences can be pleasurable, neutral, or painful.
    - ▹ You likely won't ever experience someone else's body, and there will always be the experience of *your* body. Remember that the body is an idea, a mental construct.
- **Does what is aware *of* the body-mind experience pleasure or pain?**
    - ▹ Does what is aware *of* the pain suffer due to the pain?
    - ▹ Is it affected by it, or is it just aware *of* it?
    - ▹ Awareness isn't affected by pleasure or pain in the body or mind. It is untouched by them; it is only aware of them.
    - ▹ Ask yourself: **Is Awareness affected in any way?**
    - ▹ Where is the pain or pleasure from a few moments ago? It no longer exists, except as a memory.

- ▷ Notice that the memory of pain doesn't include the experience of pain.

- Let's also look at psychological pain and happiness.
  - ▷ If the mind has thoughts causing psychological pain or negative emotions, **does what is aware of the thoughts and feelings suffer?**
  - ▷ If there are feelings of happiness, is what is aware of those feelings affected?
  - ▷ **You**, Awareness, never suffer. **You**, pure Aliveness, are always free of suffering, pain, fear, doubt, and problems.
  - ▷ Check for yourself whether this is true.

- **You**, Awareness, are also never affected or addicted to feeling pleasure or being happy. Check this as well.

- **You** are uncaused peace, ease, wholeness, and freedom.

AWARENESS

How far can *You* open up?

- Take a breath and relax.
- **Like a camera zooming out, let your attention open wide, as wide as it will go.**
    - ▹ Un-focus from (take attention off) any thoughts, feelings, sensations, sights, or sounds.
    - ▹ Like zooming out on your computer screen, allow attention to go as wide as it will go. Let everything be.
    - ▹ Allow everything to appear exactly as it is, but don't focus on anything in particular. Zoom out as far as attention will go.
    - ▹ Attention will quickly zoom in and focus on something again like a thought or feeling. When you notice, again relax your attention and zoom out to include everything all at once.
    - ▹ Notice that attention spontaneously zooms in again and focuses on content. Notice that the intention to zoom out also occurs spontaneously.

- Knowingly be the wide-open, zoomed-out attention in which everything is included for as long as it naturally occurs.

- Notice that when attention is wide open, the aware Presence that was already there is more obvious.
    - **Be this Awareness already aware of everything,** including the body, thoughts, sensations, and even the idea of a self.
    - This is choiceless, open, aware Knowing.

- **All experiences (internal, like thoughts, and external, like objects and people) appear within and as this Presence.**
    - Freedom is knowing that you are this open, aware Knowing.
    - Freedom is not about remaining like this or abiding in this!
    - This always already aware Presence is **You.**

You Are Not Your Body

Consider that the experience of a body may be like the experience of being in a car. You *get in* and feel like you're inside it. You use it to experience going places, but it's not what you are. **You** are not your body just as you are not your car.

Consider that you may be wearing the body as you wear clothes. A body is a temporary covering to experience life with. But **You** are not your clothes.

Consider that the body changes all the time. How can *You* be what is constantly changing?

Long ago you identified with the body-form. Now you're strongly attached to it. Could it be that **You** never became the body? That **You** are what was there before the body? That **You** were never born, **You** are not the body now, and that although the body dies **You** never die? **You** never merged with or became a body.

Right now, **You** are already everything all at once.

Consider that **You** may have never become the projection but have always been the projector. Simultaneously, there is the experience of/through a so-called body. Consider that **You** are not in the body but that the body (and all bodies) appear in **You**.

The experience of a body continues until death. We seem to experience a unique, local body. However, the word *body* is a concept, shorthand for a bundle of constantly shifting sensations. We've made this concept into an object, leading us to believe it exists. But the body is never more than a mental concept.

What It's Like to See This

Do you have memories of out-of-body experiences in childhood? Many people do. Somehow we were not yet so stuck within the illusory borders of our bodies. The body seemed much more fluid because the concept hadn't become so rigid yet.

When it's seen that we are not the set of sensations that we call a body, this doesn't mean our experience changes. We still feel like we're living life from within it. At the same time, there is no doubt that the body as a concept is an illusion.

The sensations are real. When there is a pain sensation in what I call my foot, there will be thoughts and actions to do something about it. But this happens spontaneously, as a natural reaction. This is not about denying or ignoring real, felt experience. We are not trying to deny or dissociate from the body.

The body takes care of itself. Thoughts and actions arise to feed it, move it, and relax it—or not. Some body-minds don't do this successfully. The point is that no one in the body is making it happen. **You**—the alive

Awareness experiencing the bundle of shifting sensations we call *body*—are never affected.

When we've looked closely enough, we realize that we never experience a body as a whole. We never experience a self inside a body either. This frees us from our obsession with the body and from any need to manipulate its experience.

Now *my body,* a bundle of constantly shifting sensations, simply arises in experience. When something needs to be done about it, actions occur spontaneously. When there is hunger, the body finds food to eat. When there is pain, natural actions arise to deal with it. When there is pleasure, it's enjoyed as long as it lasts. But there is no belief in the concept of *my body* anymore.

THE AUTHOR OR DOER

Do you control the thoughts or actions of the body?

- **Would anything stop happening if you stopped thinking about (doing) it?**
  - ▹ Please consider this deeply.
  - ▹ Do thoughts just appear, or do you make them appear?
  - ▹ If you don't think about doing something (e.g., going shopping later) does the body still do that thing?
  - ▹ What about the actions of the body? Does the body just move, or do you have to *make it* move?
  - ▹ Notice how and when the body moves. Is it always preceded by thought?
  - ▹ Do you move the leg or the arm? Or does it just move, often along with the thought that it should move? Why do *you* move the leg but not beat the heart?
- **We're brainwashed into believing that we're doing our lives:** that we're doing the thinking, making (some) actions of the body happen, and are in charge of choosing and deciding. **But is there really a doer or author of any of it?**

- ▹ Don't thoughts and actions (including choices and decisions) happen spontaneously, whether we think about them or not, whether we feel like we will them to or not?
- ▹ You've been told since birth that you're a self and that this self has agency and free will. It makes things happen.
- ▹ But there is no one making things happen. Thoughts simply appear in the body-mind, actions of the body just happen, and choices are made without a controller.
- ▹ If you had any control, you could *make* thoughts and actions appear or disappear. You can do neither.

- There is no self to have a will, free or not.
    - ▹ **Test this in direct experience until it becomes clear.**
    - ▹ Check with small and big thoughts, minor and major actions, and easy and complex choices.

THE AUTHOR OR DOER

Are you making seeing, hearing, or sensing happen?

- Right now, there is hearing, there is seeing, and there is sensing. **Are you doing anything to make these things happen?**
    - ▹ Are you causing any of it?
    - ▹ Are you making anything at all happen?
- Listen to a sound. Is there anyone doing the hearing? Or does the hearing just happen?
- Look at an object. Is the looking just happening or is there someone doing the looking?
- What is doing the rain? What is doing the beating of the heart? What is doing the breathing? What is dividing the cells? What is doing your life?
- Isn't life just living itself?
- Isn't the body-mind just being done?
- It's not "I am thinking." Thinking is arising.
- It's not "I am seeing, hearing, or sensing." It's simply hearing, seeing, and sensing happening.
- Awareness doesn't *do* anything. It's the background against which and within which everything arises and unfolds. Thinking about it won't make it clearer. It is beyond thought.

- **You** are what is aware *of* this spontaneous unfolding.
- **Just keep noticing: Is anything not spontaneously arising? Is there a personal author or doer of any of it?**
    - ▹ You've never created a thought or sensation, produced a feeling, made an action happen, made a choice or decision occur, or prevented it from occurring.
    - ▹ **You** are the Presence in which a spontaneous, complex set of psychosomatic biochemical processes unfolds.
    - ▹ How can you say you make anything happen? Do you make molecules cross cell membranes? Do you make synapses transmit?
- **You are being done. You are being lived.**

THE AUTHOR OR DOER

Without a doer, can there be (self-) judgment?

- **Without control over actions, thoughts, or sensations, what are we basing our judgments on?**
    - ▹ How can we judge ourselves or others for (not) doing something if we have no control over either thoughts or actions?
    - ▹ If I am not the doer and there is no one to have free will, then there is no personal responsibility. And that is true for everyone alive.
    - ▹ **How can we then judge anyone for any thought or action?**
    - ▹ How can there be pride or shame for the things we think or do?
    - ▹ Notice that you can't decide not to judge, either!
    - ▹ If this is seen clearly, judging becomes absurd all by itself.
- We feel so strongly that there is control and personal responsibility. But that doesn't make it true! This feeling is based on conditioned beliefs.
- Isn't the only possible spontaneous result of knowing this a deep compassion for everyone?

    - This doesn't mean we accept everything and don't act. It means we no longer designate people or ourselves as "wrong" or "bad."
    - Notice that this applies to spiritual progress or understanding as well.

- It's not up to you how much you see, inquire, understand, or integrate. It's not up to you how long or deeply you get stuck in emotions and thoughts. It's not up to you when or whether you have any insights. That is all just spontaneously unfolding as well!

- **Judgment about this understanding is also absurd.**

- **There is no *you* making the understanding happen or not.**

AWARENESS

Is there anyone *doing* Awareness?

- **Is anyone doing the *being aware*?**
- **Is anyone doing Presence or Aliveness?**
    - ▹ Investigate and see: **You** already *are* aware.
- Awareness is always already there. It comes first and it just *is*, uncaused. There are no conditions for it to appear.
    - ▹ Check this in first-person experience.
- There is no you, separate from Presence.
    - ▹ **You** are the Awareness, the Aliveness, already.
    - ▹ Aware Presence is effortless and uncaused.
- **It's important to see that this is not a personal awareness. There is no one there to own it!**
    - ▹ Body-minds don't have private awarenesses.
    - ▹ It's one spontaneous, alive, all-encompassing Awareness.
    - ▹ The Aliveness is already there. Body-minds appear within it.
- **It's also impossible to be more aware.**

- There's no you to do Awareness, so there's no you to be more or less aware. Awareness *is* **You.**

- **What if you completely forgot about the self?**
    - If the sense of a *me* is completely ignored, is the expression of life any different?
    - Forget your self, lose your self, lose the doer: Does anything change?

- **Are you really a somebody if life carries on exactly as before when there is no thinking about a someone?**
    - Just as no one does Awareness, no one does inquiry.
    - No one makes an interest in nonduality or inquiry happen.
    - Inquiry does itself. It's spontaneous. So if a long time passes without inquiry or progress, it's not because you're doing something wrong. That's just how it's naturally unfolding.

You Are Not the Doer

Consider that if no one is doing Aliveness and it is uncaused, this means that Awareness is *free*. The body-mind appears in this free uncaused Awareness that **You** already are.

Consider that there is no doer, no volitional agent, no one in control of the body-mind. No matter how often the thought or feeling comes up that you are the doer, this does not change the fact that you're not. It's just a very strong, recurring belief.

You don't create the thought that you are the doer; it just appears. This in itself is further proof that you're not the doer! Nothing we think of or believe in changes reality. Consider that the beliefs that we're in control, that we make things happen, or that we have responsibility have been programmed into us since childhood.

Judgment, guilt, and morality are social constructs. All rest on the assumption that you are in charge of (certain parts of) your thoughts and actions. When this is seen to be untrue, you don't turn into an immoral couch potato. The conditioning and programming continue in the body-mind just as before. Only the thoughts *judging* the behavior are no longer believed.

Consider that **You** are what is aware of the actions, choices, and thoughts happening in and through the body-mind. That includes thinking about reading this book, doing the inquiry, and gaining any understanding. All of that is unfolding spontaneously!

Consider that knowing there is no doer does not put an end to feelings, thoughts, or actions. No doer only means there is no one making them happen. Often, actions and feelings can even become more intense because there's no self in the way. There can now be integration of Awareness and body-mind. We are both. And we continue to care about life, deeply. But we do this without needing anything from it or needing to know why it is so.

What It's Like to See This

Truly seeing the absence of the doer is the end of psychological stress and suffering. But it's also the most difficult insight in this book. Not because it's difficult to see per se, but because the belief in it is so tenacious. It's the essence of the separate self.

When we see this, we know for sure that we are being lived. There are deeds but no doer, thoughts but no thinker. We're a set of constantly unfolding psychosomatic processes, embedded within much larger, more complex systems. Believing we can somehow create separation and distance from the larger system on our tiny island of selfhood is quite absurd.

Nothing I think or do is up to me or because of me. Writing these words is as spontaneous as a heart beating or cells dividing. I am not making it happen and have no control over it happening. I may have thoughts that create the illusion that I'm the one making it happen. But when I look without beliefs, it's clear that those thoughts are also spontaneous.

No matter where we look, we can't find a separate author of any part of our lives. This insight alone brings vast freedom. What is there to worry about if I can't make it (not) happen? Why should I stress about it?

This is not the same as saying there's no free will. Free will is a concept. It requires a separate self to have it. There is no self and no one to have free will, so the problem no longer exists. Before we knew about free will or personal responsibility, life just happened. If we lose our sense of agency due to psychiatric conditions, for example, life continues to happen. There may be a feeling of having free will. This feeling may be very strong. But even that feeling comes and goes. **You** remain as the Awareness of it.

AWARENESS

Is there anything substantial in experience?

- *Is anything we experience substantial?*
    - ▹ Are there any separate entities or objects *out there* beyond our concepts of them?
    - ▹ How would you prove something is substantial?
    - ▹ There is nothing substantial in experience. At the same time, there's always already a continual stream of Aliveness.
    - ▹ You can't filter Presence out from experience because it has no substance and it's not a thing.
- **We *thingify* reality.**
    - ▹ All we have are our raw sensory perceptions.
    - ▹ Don't things only exist in language, in our names for them?
    - ▹ Without naming anything, there is only a seamless, formless appearance of sensory perceptions from the sense organs (images, sounds, feelings, thoughts, etc.).
    - ▹ Check to see if this is true.

- **Take a moment to look around. Now drop all labels for anything occurring in experience.**
    - ▹ Drop the label of *dropping labels* as well.
    - ▹ If any new concept comes up, drop the label for that too.
    - ▹ Notice that there is no self to be found in this appearance either. If the label *self* comes up, drop that label.
- Take the position of there not being any separate things and there not being a separate self. See how experience shows up from that position.
- **You can't get into it and you can't get out of it because *You already are it.***
- This ever-present Awareness is more substantial than the insubstantial content appearing within it, as it is always there, while all so-called *things* come and go.

SEPARATE

Where is the border between inner and outer?

- **Where does *me* end and *the rest of the world* begin?**
  - ▹ Where is the dividing line between myself and not myself?
  - ▹ It's impossible to find where *me* ends and the world begins.
- In a previous inquiry, we tried to find a border to the body. Here, we're looking more generally.
- **Can there be an interior and exterior if there is no dividing line?**
  - ▹ Try right now to find this separation in direct experience.
  - ▹ Everything appears seamlessly, but thinking adds in division where none actually exists.
  - ▹ There is only a seamless whole, aware Awareness.
- For example, the mind says the table is *over there.*
  - ▹ Does this mean the experience of the table is over there?
  - ▹ Or is the experience of the table neither here nor there but in Awareness?

- Is there a separation between the table and the experience of the table? Is there a division between what I call *me* and the experience of the table?

- **Where are all these boundaries (here, there, inner, outer, table, me) that we speak of all the time?**

- Is everyday experience really one of separation?

    - Then why did we have to learn about separation as children?

    - **What, besides thoughts, indicates actual separation?** That there are sensations here? That there are supposed facts of space and distance? That there are supposed objects?

- Whenever and wherever we look without concepts or thinking, all we find is a seamless whole.

    - We can find no boundaries of any kind.

    - This ordinary experience is already one!

SEPARATE

Is there anything behind your eyes?

- When you point anywhere in the world you point at appearances that seem separate from you, the one pointing.
    - ▹ Direct your attention to various things in the room right now by pointing at them one by one.
    - ▹ Do this before reading on.
- Now point to where others see your face: Take your index finger and point it at yourself.
    - ▹ **What is the finger pointing to?**
    - ▹ We are turning attention around 180 degrees from objects out there to the subject, the place you're looking out of.
    - ▹ Do you find a space of pure Awareness?
    - ▹ An empty, clear, transparent, self-evidently awake space?
    - ▹ At the same time, this experience is still full of everything happening: the finger-pointing, the scene beyond, sensations, thoughts. . . . But the looking is now from the Awareness in which it's all happening.

- ▹ What do you find? Are you also looking out of this wide open, crystal clear Awareness?[2]

- What we expect the finger to point at when we point at our face is *me*, the separate self.

  - ▹ **But we don't find anything. The self is only an idea.**
  - ▹ If there is no self in here, are there any others out there?
  - ▹ Isn't everyone (everything) appearing in **You**, as **You**?

---

2. This inquiry is adapted from The Headless Way. You can find more experiments like this at *headless.org*.

SEPARATE

What makes something *mine* or *not mine*?

- We call the body "my" body. Sometimes we call other people and things mine, as in "my husband" or "my car."
    - ▹ **When does it stop making sense to say something is mine?**
    - ▹ See how arbitrary this is? We mentally divide the world into self/other, inside/outside. This division is not there in reality!
    - ▹ It's not *my* body but a body. They are not *my* thoughts or sensations; they are spontaneous arisings.
    - ▹ **It is not *my* experience; it is a unique experience that arises in an impersonal aware Presence.**
- First, there is pure experience—*this*, exactly as it is. Between ages one and three, we learn to make it about *me*.
    - ▹ Now it becomes *my* seeing, *my* hearing, *my* sensing. It becomes *my* body, *my* feelings, *my* actions, *my* thoughts. We even learn they are *my* relationships and *my* things.
    - ▹ We learn that it's *my* life—*my* little piece of *this*.

    - ▹ Look right now: isn't there just experience, exactly as it is?

- **Why do I experience my body and thoughts, but not yours?**
    - ▹ Remove the label *mine* and it's clear. There is an experience of sensations and thoughts which seem local and unique. We add the concept of a self and make it personal. Now they are *my thoughts and sensations* instead of just an experience.
- **What is aware *of* experience is universal.** One impersonal Aliveness experiencing 8 billion local experiences.
- Awareness can seem personal if we believe that I have my awareness and you have yours. That's not the Awareness we're talking about. That's your body-mind's attention or focus.
- **The Aliveness that *I am* is not mine, because there is no self to own it.**
- All body-minds appear in what *I am*. Everything appears in the same Awareness.

AWARENESS

Isn't *this* a nondual experience right now?

- **Why do you assume you're not experiencing non-duality now?**
    - ▹ What is a nondual experience supposed to be like?
    - ▹ We may believe it will feel like we are one with everything. But apart from drug-induced states, this type of experience rarely occurs.
    - ▹ **Experience is always through and as a body-mind.**
    - ▹ I'll never experience you or a tree. Experience is individual.
- **However, Awareness is aware of everything.**
    - ▹ It's one Awareness having your experience and my experience.
    - ▹ Imagine 8 billion fingers on the same hand. Imagine 8 billion cells of one organism. The finger and cell *experience* feels separate, but they aren't really separate from the whole.
    - ▹ The idea that we'll someday experience oneness is a belief. It makes this experience feel like it's not enough and creates a sense of lack.

- **Look out at the world as though you're newly born.**
    - ▹ Everything is completely new. You have no name or words for anything. You have no memories. It's one gigantic display.
    - ▹ Thoughts will come up. Ignore them as best you can. Let all the narration in your head be without listening to it.
    - ▹ Keep returning to the shiny newness and inexplicable, unnamable reality of experience.
- **Where, in all of this, are *you*?**
    - ▹ Isn't everything just appearing?
    - ▹ Without thinking, is there a *you* here?
    - ▹ Look again but not as a person—simply sights, sounds, and sensations happening. Not happening *to* someone, just happening.
    - ▹ Can you see that the self is just a thought?
- **What about *this* is not enlightened?**
    - ▹ Without thinking, what is this moment lacking?

AWARENESS

Is aware Presence a thing or object?

- **Is aware Aliveness separate from the body-mind?**
  - ▹ Is it found anywhere else other than right here?
  - ▹ Can you point to it? Can you look at it as a separate thing? Or can it only be recognized as what already *is*?
- **You can't point to it or see it because You *are it*.**
  - ▹ This may seem to contradict earlier inquiries. That's the paradox that occurs when we try to illustrate these concepts with language.
  - ▹ It's like teeth trying to bite themselves or an eyeball trying to see itself. **Aware Presence is what is being aware.**
  - ▹ You can't be aware of Awareness—Awareness is already there and aware of the attempt to be aware of it.
  - ▹ We're not talking about some special, spiritual Awareness or higher Consciousness. We're talking about the ordinary, alive Presence that is already here now.

- The alive Presence that is **You** has no form and is not an object. We can't say much about it because it is empty, formless, and without content.
    - ▹ It can't be understood by thinking about it. It can't be perceived as a sensation, state, or feeling. But it is doubtlessly present. **We can only be it, knowingly.**
    - ▹ If you only focus on thoughts, sensations, or achieving and abiding in specific states, you will never discover it.
- **You already are it. Now you know this.**
    - ▹ Awareness knows itself completely. We already are what we were seeking. It can't be lost.
    - ▹ Since it's not something separate from us, we can't get deeper into it, stabilize in it, or embody it. We already are it!
- **You cannot become more You.**

You Are Not Separate

Consider that there is no *me* on the one hand and an Awareness on the other hand for *me* to get to. The sense of subject-object separation is so strong that this belief in Awareness as an object is very sticky.

Consider that there is no little me and big me, no small separate self and true self, no wave and ocean, no cloud and sky. These are all analogies used initially to help us realize we're not limited to being one person. But they are only to make a point. Ultimately, there is no separation at all. There is only sky. There is only ocean. There is only Knowing. The subject-object divide drops away when we truly look.

Consider that the appearances (the content) change all the time, but this changing content is simultaneously the container. This is almost impossible to put into language because words objectify. Reality is both form and formlessness at the same time. There is no separation between container and content.

There is only ocean appearing as waves. It looks like separate waves, but it is all the same Ocean. The ten thousand things we seem to see out there are neither in here nor out there because there is no inside or outside. We are not the subjects experiencing these objects. Subjects and objects are one.

Consider that the mind will never understand this. In that sense, it remains a mystery. At the same time, without adding any concepts or thinking, there is a seamless multidimensional ocean of experience that is simultaneously the experiencer. What you're looking at is **You**! There is no separate you.

Another way of saying this is that everything is the same energy or consciousness taking on different forms. None of it is a solid, separate object or subject. It is one. Separation is only an idea.

What It's Like to See This

We mentally *add* separation to reality. So, when separation is seen to be false, we continue to experience the same reality but are no longer fooled by the cognitive illusion of separation. When this is clear, we no longer see other people as separate from us.

For example: When I meet you, understanding that separation is false, there is no longer an added idea that you are *other than me*. The idea no longer comes up. It feels like meeting myself in a different form. What I say to you, I am saying to myself. What you say to me, you are saying to yourself, which is also me. It feels more like a sharing of different forms of being than a meeting of two separate individuals.

This is not the same as liking everyone. Due to the conditioning of the body-mind, we can still dislike another person's behavior while simultaneously understanding that this is not a separate person. Similarly, this doesn't mean I passively accept all behavior. The body-mind still reacts to the behavior of others. But none of this involves a separate self!

Another way of saying this is that meeting and relating with others now takes place from Presence instead of from the position of a separate self. And it is always in the here and *now*, without the addition of ego. This makes relating vastly simpler and easier. We have effectively removed one side of the ego barrier in the relationship.

But as with everything in this book, these results are not due to a self achieving something. They are the natural, organic results of inquiry. In other words, trying to get here won't work, because that would be the illusory self trying to do so. This can only be achieved by seeing clearly what we are, and by knowing that there is no separation.

AWARENESS

Is there a separate observer or witness?

- Sometimes we come to believe that Awareness is the observer or witness element of our experience. This is yet another concept that we have heard or read about elsewhere. Let's examine it in direct experience.

- **If you look for an observer or witness, can you find such an entity?**

    - ▹ Look right now. Where is the observer or witness?

    - ▹ All we ever find is a *sense* of something observing.

    - ▹ But is this sense always there? Isn't the observer or witness another sensation that comes and goes?

- Sometimes it feels like there is a witness or observer, and at other times we don't have this sensation. Thankfully, we're not constantly self-consciously witnessing our lives!

- **What is aware of the sense that there is an observer or witness to life?**

    - ▹ If it is a sensation that comes and goes, and if there is Awareness *of* it, then it can't be what **You** essentially are.

- ▹ The observer or witness is yet another appearance that comes and goes in **You**.
- ▹ Check this with your direct experience until it becomes clear.

me THE SENSE OF BEING A SELF

If you look right now, is there a *me* anywhere?

- **Focus on the feeling or sense of *me*.**
    - ▹ Close your eyes and try to feel the sense of being a person.
    - ▹ Notice how constricted and limited that feels.
    - ▹ Now recognize the aware Presence that is aware of this feeling or sense of *me*.
    - ▹ Notice the expansion that is immediately available.
- **Anything experienced is not You.**
    - ▹ It's something that appears to **You**. It is content.
    - ▹ Even the sense of consciousness comes and goes.
    - ▹ It is absent during deep sleep and while under anesthesia, for example.
    - ▹ The sense of self comes and goes many times a day when we experience flow or when we are so present for another that we forget ourselves.

   - ▹ What is always present, however, is Awareness.

- **How do you know (what evidence is there) that experience is happening to a separate you?**
   - ▹ Can you observe an experiencer? Or is there just experience?
   - ▹ Life isn't personal. It's not my experience. It's just experience.
   - ▹ There may be a fear that you'll disappear without a sense of self. Is that fear always there? You still exist, even when the fear is not there.
   - ▹ **Can an illusion disappear?**

- **Where is the self in all this?**
   - ▹ The self is an assumption. There is no me.
   - ▹ The only thing keeping us invested in the self is the belief that it is real.

me THE SENSE OF BEING A SELF

Is the sense of *me* always there, or does it come and go?

- This concept is so important that we'll go through it again: **If the feeling of me comes and goes, it can't be you, can it?** That would mean you disappear whenever you're not having the sensation.

- **What is aware of the sense of self?**

    - ▹ If the sense of self appears to **You**, it can't be *You*.

    - ▹ Look everywhere, inside and outside. Can you find a self?

    - ▹ If you're a self, then you should be able to find one!

    - ▹ Is the sense of a self anything more than a recurring thought?

- **Notice that there is *never* a direct experience of a self.**

    - ▹ Trying to look for a *me* is like playing hide-and-seek with a ghost. The self is an idea hiding out in your mind.

    - ▹ No matter how intensely you seek it, you will never find it.

    - ▹ All you will find are thoughts and feelings *about* a self.

- **Can the "I" thought do anything?** Can a thought think or act?
    - ▹ The sense of self comes with thinking and is itself a thought!
    - ▹ The "I" thought and all thoughts about it (What should I do? Who should I be? etc.) do not refer to anyone.
    - ▹ ***I* or *me* doesn't refer to an actual entity.**
- **Do we have to eliminate a sense of self if it doesn't exist?**
    - ▹ Can we get rid of something that doesn't exist?
    - ▹ The sense of being a *me* will keep arising. It most likely won't stop until you die.
    - ▹ We're not trying to get rid of it.
    - ▹ We're only seeing that it isn't what we are.

You Are Not a Self

Consider that the sense of there being a *me* comes and goes. It arises, hangs around for a while, and disappears in **You**. Before you learned the concept of self, you already existed. A baby doesn't have a sense of self and yet there they are, existing anyway!

Consider that everything you think about yourself is just another thought about a nonexistent character. There is a body, and there are thoughts. But remember, thoughts about *me* are like thoughts about Sherlock Holmes. Thinking thoughts about Sherlock Holmes doesn't make him real. And thoughts about Sherlock Holmes do not refer to a real person.

Self-referencing thoughts constitute a mental loop. These are thoughts and more thoughts, all referring to a central thought, the "I" thought. The sense of being a self is no more real than these thoughts. It is part of that same loop.

Consider that once again, nothing needs to be done about the sense of being a self. Some believe strongly that they need to tame the self, undo the self, or even kill the self. None of that is true. There is no separate *me* to do any of that or to do it to. No separate *me* could make these things happen.

Consider again that you already existed before you knew you were a separate self. And if you get amnesia or for some other reason lose your sense of *me*, you continue to exist anyway. The *me* is mentally added onto existence, onto the alive Presence that is already there, experiencing life.

This is the essence of the misidentification with a separate self. It is nothing more than an additional, optional cognitive filter that we have come to believe constitutes the truth of our being.

But the sense of self is simply a mistaken identity.

What It's Like to See This

There is no fat spider-me sitting at the center of life's web. The sense of being *me*, the sense of self, comes and goes like any other sensation. **You** are what is aware of the me-sensation. When this is seen, you continue to feel like an individual. But now you know: just because it feels that way doesn't mean it's true.

For decades we've learned to focus on that feeling, give all our attention to it, and believe we were limited to it. Now you can know that everything, including the sense of "me," appears and disappears in what **You** are.

The human experience is an experience of duality. We're going to be living the life of a body-mind until the body dies. At the same time, we can be absolutely certain that we're not limited to a self housed inside a body. We're free from the limitations of an illusory self while experiencing a normal human life.

This is why nothing in experience changes due to a nondual understanding. The experience remains the same, although its quality changes. It can't be repeated often enough. The experience here is the same as the experience of any other person. There is no *experience* of oneness here. However, there is a crystal clear *knowing* of oneness and no-self. It is doubtless that there is no person to be found.

This results in freedom from identification with an illusory self, so there is no further interest in or obsession with such a self. There isn't the slightest interest in promoting or defending the illusion. The character simply unfolds and does what it does.

The idea of self appears and disappears. Even though there are thoughts about a self, they are no longer believed.

AWARENESS

Are *You* ever not here?

- **Is there ever a time when You are not present?** Is there any moment when **You** don't exist?
- Even when we feel trapped in dense clouds of thought and feelings, there has to be Awareness in order to experience these.
- Is that true? Look in direct experience.
- **If you are supposedly "lost in thought," that is always already being experienced by You, Awareness.**
- If there is confusion, doubt, or the belief that *this is not it*, there has to be an aware Presence to know that.
- If there is the thought that *Awareness is not here now*, it is Awareness that is aware of that thought.
- **Awareness is already aware!** This is not about a better, deeper, or more expansive experience.
- **You are never not here. You are always here *now*.** This is probably the only thing that is ever certain.
    - ▹ The misunderstanding about falling out of it (seeing it and not seeing it, catching glimpses, etc.) comes from the belief that there is a separate someone who can remain

aware of Awareness. But there is no self that needs to be aware of Awareness. There is only Awareness, already aware of itself.

- Before the body was supposedly born, **You** already existed.
- When the identification with the body-mind goes, it is clear that **You** always were, **You** always are, and **You** always will be.
    - ▹ There is no self that must be seen through or needs to die. There never was a self to begin with. It was just a thought.
    - ▹ **You are always already here and free of the self.**
- Knowing what **You** are and that **You** always are, it is clear there is no self for you to be.

LOCATED IN SPACE / TIME

When is it ever not *now*? When are we not in the *now*?

- **Where is time when you're not thinking about it?**
  - ▹ Does time exist if there are no thoughts about the past, the future, or the passing of time itself?
  - ▹ Is it possible to be anywhere other than *now*?
  - ▹ You can have thoughts about the past or the future, but these thoughts are occurring *now*.
  - ▹ You can imagine the past or future, but that is occurring *now*.
- **It is always, eternally *now*. *Now* is eternal (not in time).**
  - ▹ The past and future don't exist except in thought.
  - ▹ Now is another name for **You** (Awareness).
  - ▹ Whenever aware Aliveness is recognized, there is only *now*.
- To experience time there must be thinking. When we recognize ourselves as what is aware of thought, time disappears.

- ▹ **It is *now* that we are free and awake,** not in some imaginary past or future. The interest in an imagined future awakening falls away.
- ▹ The belief in becoming more awake over time dissolves.

- **If there is only *now*, did anything ever happen?**
  - ▹ Memories about the past happen *now*.
  - ▹ Ideas about the future happen *now*.
  - ▹ Without believing the content (thought) there is no time.
  - ▹ Where is yesterday *now*? Where is tomorrow *now*?
- Realizing there is only *now*, we can be finished with interest in the past or future.
  - ▹ The interest in a personal history or future falls away, even if thoughts about them continue to arise.
  - ▹ **Without a personal history, there is no separate self.**
- Now **You** are free.

LOCATED IN SPACE / TIME

What is not included in *this*?

- **Is there anything else beyond *this*?**
    - ▹ Where would that be? What could that be?
    - ▹ There is nothing hidden behind *this*. We don't have to unveil anything or uncover a secret.
    - ▹ That's why it's *shining in plain view* and *the open secret*.
- **Is anything not included or not accepted in *this*?**
    - ▹ How could that be if it's *this* already?
    - ▹ *This* is all-inclusive. Nothing is excluded from or unacceptable about *this* except in our thinking!
- ***This* is always already it.**
- **All we can say is, *this is*.**
    - ▹ Everything else is a concept added onto *this*.
    - ▹ *This* hides nothing from us.
    - ▹ ***This* has no intrinsic reason, meaning, or cause and effect.** Those are additions our minds came up with.

    - ▹ Everything you can dream up is already included in *this*.

- **We are always already *this*.**
    - ▹ *This* is Awareness itself, without content, time, or location.
    - ▹ We can't talk about what *this* is because it is nondual. *This* isn't anything substantial; it is no-thing.
    - ▹ We can't know it as we know information, because we *are* it.
    - ▹ *This*, like *now*, is another term for **You**.

- ***This* is already 100 percent awake, enlightened, and liberated.**
    - ▹ Our beliefs that *this* can't be it—it's not good enough, it's not what I think it should be—are the only things blocking our direct knowing of *this*.

LOCATED IN SPACE / TIME

Where are *You*? Is there a location to *You*?

- **Can you find a location or a center to You?**
    - ▹ If it feels like you're behind the eyes, what is aware of that?
    - ▹ Does what is aware of that feeling have a location?
- **Can you find an end to Awareness?**
    - ▹ Close your eyes and imagine going to the very edge of Awareness. Travel to the end of Awareness. Keep going farther and farther and try to get to the end of it.
    - ▹ If there is an end, shouldn't we be able to experience it?
    - ▹ Don't think about this—try to *do* it, to experience it.
    - ▹ Isn't wherever you are always here?
    - ▹ We can imagine an end to Awareness conceptually, in our minds. But we can't experience such an end.
    - ▹ Awareness has no center and no location.
- It is not located in space because it is not an object.
- It is what all space appears within or as.

- The concepts of time and space do not apply to Awareness because **Awareness is what space-time appears within.**
    - ▹ Space-time is conceptual knowledge created by the mind. Before we learned about space-time, it didn't exist.
    - ▹ Space and time are constructs inherent to the human sense organs, which are the *headset* through which we experience the world. But space and time are not fundamental to reality.
    - ▹ Just as the sense of being a self is a filter, space and time are filters we are programmed to add to reality.[3]

---

3. The theory that space-time is not fundamental to reality but part of our human headset is proposed by cognitive scientist Donald D. Hoffman in his book *The Case Against Reality: How Evolution Hid the Truth from Our Eyes* (Penguin, 2020).

You Are

We've now seen that everything that appears—the entire external and internal world of experience, is what **You** are not. We've undone six layers of beliefs about a separate self that doesn't exist to reveal what we are at our core.

Whatever you can experience is an object, an appearance, and not what **You** are. **You** are what experiences. You are the seer, not the seen. Without the seer there wouldn't even be a world to experience.

We've gone through all these layers of what could constitute a separate self and have found them empty of substance. We've thoroughly explored what we are not. If any of this is unclear, go back to those inquiries and look again. Undoing belief in these layers takes time (although time is an illusion). Which of and when these layers are seen through depends on the conditioning of your particular body-mind.

Remember: **You** can't be anything that appears to **You**. **You** can't be anything that comes and goes.

It should now be quite clear that **You** are not a separate self. **You** never were separate and will never be separate. **You** are the alive, aware Presence that knows the experience of the body-mind. There is no self in the picture. If that's not clear, go back to the inquiries and investigate again. It takes as long as it takes.

This goes against decades of conditioning and societal programming. Know that these deep-seated automatic beliefs will likely continue to arise no matter how completely they have been proven to be false.

Consider that the arising of an old, conditioned belief is not a problem—unless there is another belief that it is a problem!

What It's Like to See This

This understanding of no-self can be disorienting and that can bring up fear. Notice that feelings of disorientation or fear are nothing more than further appearances coming and going in the aware Presence of **You**. For the body-mind writing this book, there was a period of intense fear. It passed.

If it's clear that there is no separate self, there is no reason left to be interested in one. The interest in the personal me, its history, its needs and desires, its "poor me" and "great me" stories . . . none of it hooks us anymore.

This leads to a natural unwinding of the obsession with selfing, much as the blades of a fan come to a complete stop after switching it off. It often takes some time to notice that this is unfolding. It slowly (and sometimes quickly) becomes clear that whole areas of past obsession no longer arise in the mind.

The guilt, pride, stress, and worry about an imaginary past and future may fall away first. Then, further areas of thinking about the self can stop arising. We can imagine these as knots or clumps of sticky thoughts. There is the knot of personality, the knot of relationships, or the knot of goals and ambitions. Over time, these knots dissolve, but we only notice this in retrospect.

At some point, there is almost no self-referential thinking left. No thinking about the self or character arises in consciousness. Most thinking is purely practical: what to buy at the supermarket, what to wear for this weather, or what to discuss in a meeting.

Experience continues to show up through the body-mind. The experience here continues to feel unique and separate. But it is happening to no one.

There's more on this in the final chapter.

AWARENESS

Fall into *You*.

- We now come to three variations of Awareness Inquiries that may seem like meditations. But it's crucial to understand that they're *not* mindfulness meditations. There's no need to make this a daily sitting practice unless that's what you want to do.
    - ▹ Read through them and try them as you are spontaneously drawn to them. Frequency and time spent don't matter.
    - ▹ These are about recognizing what **You** already are. Don't expect anything to happen! Read more about this at the end of this section.
- Sit comfortably somewhere quiet and look around. Notice ordinary, everyday Awareness looking out through the eyes.
    - ▹ Close the eyes and notice the same Awareness is still there.
    - ▹ Remain as this open, formless field of non-dual Awareness.
    - ▹ Your eyes can remain closed or open and unfocused; both are fine.
- When attention is drawn to an object, **ignore the object (let it be) and return to formless Awareness.**

- ▹ An object is any thought, sensation, idea, memory, feeling, vision, or state—even beautiful insights or immense fear. Content means any content, no matter what it is.
- ▹ Remember that Awareness isn't an alternative object to put attention on. It's already there as the container of all.
- ▹ As soon as attention on an object is noticed, unhook from it and return to open, formless, objectless Awareness. Drop any thoughts or sensations like a hot coal and return to silence.

- This is about recognizing **You** over and over, not keeping the mind empty for as long as possible.
    - ▹ Every object is an opportunity to *turn around* and notice the objectless field of alive Presence already there.
    - ▹ The ability to return to Awareness will strengthen over time.
    - ▹ Once familiar, this inquiry can be done anywhere.

AWARENESS

Stand as *You*.

- This second Awareness Inquiry is about taking a stand. The principle is the same as the first inquiry, but the alternate wording may have a different effect.
- Like the other two versions, this is not an exercise to do on a fixed schedule but as often as it spontaneously occurs.
- Check right now in direct experience: Are **You** aware?
    - ▹ **You**, as Awareness, always already are.
    - ▹ This is not-two (non-dual): Awareness and **You** are the same. Your true nature is pure, aware, alive Being already.
    - ▹ **Now surrender (give up) any identification with the personal body-mind and stand as Awareness.**
    - ▹ Surrender the personal and stand as the impersonal **You**.
    - ▹ Then see how life responds to this stand.
- **Take this stand as soon as you remember and stay there for as long as it naturally occurs.**
    - ▹ No matter what is going on in experience or what reactions come up, stand as **You**.

- This means you go about the day from the stand of aware Presence while simultaneously experiencing a body-mind.
- There is a continuous surrendering of the personal and holding fast to the oneness we know we are.

- When you stand as a body, you experience separate bodies.
- When you stand as a mind, you experience separate minds.
- When you stand as Awareness, Awareness is all there is.
    - **Take "I = Awareness" as the literal truth and be it.**
    - Don't think about how to do this; just take on the intention.
- Whenever you notice yourself identifying as a body-mind, surrender that and once again stand as Awareness.
    - The ability to do this will strengthen over time.

AWARENESS

Live life as *You*.

- This is the third variation of the Awareness Inquiries, again with different wording that may have a different effect.
- Instead of identifying with a separate self, we live as what we already know we are. But we're likely not 100 percent convinced of it yet, so it's a little bit like faking it till we make it.
- To start, be without any notions, not even about Awareness.
    - ▹ Don't be a body or a mind; don't be anything at all.
    - ▹ **Be no thing. Be no one. Know nothing.**
    - ▹ Notice how all sensations and thoughts come and go.
    - ▹ Check to see whether **You** come and go. Or do you remain present and unmoving, clear and open?
- Everything is always already Awareness.
    - ▹ Notice that in being no one and identifying with Awareness, perception doesn't change, but the interpretation of perception changes.

    - Without referencing the mind, life presents itself as unitive Awareness—one seamless, spontaneous arising.

- What is, is a seamless, spontaneously unfolding whole.

- Nowhere in this oneness is a separate self ever found.

    - Live life as Awareness and see how life verifies this.

    - **Test in direct experience: Doesn't life make more sense as one, infinite, aware Presence than as a separate self?**

    - Allow this to permeate and percolate without thinking.

- Put these statements to the test: I am not the body form. I am not a constantly changing mind. I am not the thoughts or the sensations that come and go. I am not a separate self at all.

    - I am aware, alive Presence.

    - I am eternal, spacious silence.

    - I am a spontaneous unfolding in a timeless *now*.

    - I am one infinite Being.

Inquiry Is the Teacher

It may be quite difficult to engage in the Awareness Inquiries just discussed. They can seem very abstract, and you may feel a lot of resistance to them. That is okay. There is no need to force them. Just try them at least a few times.

At some point, you may find that you are doing them spontaneously. That is when inquiry has truly started to do you. It's not up to you when that happens.

Relax—inquiry evolves. Remember that you learn how to do these inquiries *by doing them*. Inquiry itself is the teacher. Don't worry and let it all unfold through you. You are not in control!

Consider that Awareness is not an object, it's the subject doing the inquiry. You will never find Awareness as an object, but the tendency is there to keep trying to do so. We try to measure progress by *finding something*. Try to let go of the idea of progress or results. Try to fall in love with Awareness Inquiry as an end in itself.

Consider returning to earlier inquiries if sticky thoughts or beliefs block you from doing the Awareness Inquiries. For example, if there are strong thoughts about there not being any progress, return to the inquiries about thinking. If there is an unshakable sense of a separate *me* in objectless Awareness, return to the inquiries about the sense of being a self. Jump back and forth among them as needed.

If we're lucky, we're pulled deeper and deeper, where the ease and freedom of Being is all there is. The light is softer and gentler here. There is no need or desire to remain in some perpetual state of Awareness. We are reminded, over and over, that Being is all there ever is.

What It's Like to See This

The tedious, pointless vacuum of no-mind wasn't where I wanted to hang out. There was nothing going on—none of my comforting drama, and no sad, defective identity to hold it all together.

But after years of running from this understanding and simultaneously wanting more of it, it finally started pulling me into itself on its own. Until one day, the so-called self became the tedious, pointless shell. And what had always seemed internal was revealed to be neither internal nor external, and also both.

Life after the realization of our true nature is ultimate freedom. There is no identification with or obsession about the body-mind, although life is still experienced as and through a body-mind. It's the same life without the psychological drama that comes up when we believe that life is about us. It's impersonal.

The more Awareness is recognized, the less interesting it becomes to pretend that we're a limited, separate self. Falling into what we are, everything happens from and with ease. We don't make any of this happen. It happens spontaneously.

We may begin to prefer the knowing of what we are over the illusion of what we are not. The Awareness Inquiries occur spontaneously. For example, we may be in the middle of a tough conversation, hotly debating an opinion we hold. Right there while speaking, the recognition occurs: What is aware? We find our body stopping mid-sentence, having lost interest in continuing the discussion. It became clear there was no one holding the opinion!

Others may notice changes in us, or they may not. Sometimes we lose some of the sharp edges of our character. Sometimes they become more pronounced! What matters is what **You** know to be true. That is what changes your world.

What is *I* or *me*? How would you describe yourself?

- Now we return to the initial, baseline question. Don't look back at your original answer just yet.
- **What are you now referring to when you say *I* or *me*?**
    - ▹ Imagine you have to explain what a human being is to an alien who magically speaks your language, or to a curious child. How would you explain now?
    - ▹ Describe this as clearly as you can.
- Compare this to the answer given at the beginning of this section. What has changed?
    - ▹ Is it clear that you are not a separate self in a body-mind?
    - ▹ Is it clear what we essentially are, our true nature? It may be impossible to put into words. Remember that clarity means no further doubts.
- **If anything is not clear, go back to the inquiry about it. An inquiry leads to different insights whenever we try it.**
    - ▹ You may now be attracted to certain inquiries more than others. Or specific inquiries

may feel more powerful than when they were first tried.

  - ▹ This changes as the beliefs about what you are change. It's not a linear process.

- Surrender and let yourself be led.
- Try to enjoy the pathless path itself.
- If you have made it this far, it can't fail.

There are no awake persons.

The awakening is to the understanding that there are no persons, there never were any persons, and there will never be persons.

You will never get enlightened.

There may be a falling away of identification with the person. And we could call that enlightenment.

The self is not liberated.

The liberation is from *belief in a self.*

Part III

Now What?

When Is Inquiry Complete?

It's common not to notice the effects of inquiry until we encounter situations that we would have resisted in the past. Sometimes others point this out to us before we notice. That is because the experience of the body-mind doesn't change due to this understanding. Instead, selfing dissolves.

Most of us bring far too many concepts and beliefs into this. We expect something to change, often radically and suddenly. We can't help it; we've read and heard too much about awakening or enlightenment. At the very least, we expect to experience more peace, joy, and happiness.

Yes, there is vastly more joy and freedom when we rediscover our true nature. But it can take a while for this to become noticeable, because the mind continues to produce belief after belief. That's our conditioning. It's like a fan continuing to turn even after someone pulls the plug.

It is done when there is no more belief in a someone who seeks, and when the impulse to seek no longer arises or is quickly seen through. This becomes obvious over time. The identification with what we are becomes more obvious and real than the misidentification with a separate self. Interest no longer goes into a self who can seek.

All that matters is this: Right now, in direct experience, is it clear what you are? It either is or it isn't. Either **You** are recognized as alive, aware Presence, or not. That is all this is ever about.

Just know **You**. When you know **You**, the search for something else or something more is over. **You** are all there is, and now this is consciously known. There is nothing left to pursue. It is doubtless *now*. It is ordinary, simple, and obvious. And it is always already the case.

I'm Not Feeling It

A huge misunderstanding about realizing our true nature is thinking that it will change our experience. We have many beliefs about what this realization is supposed to achieve. We may believe fear, jealousy, and unkindness will disappear. We may believe we will always feel happy, calm, and compassionate.

But there are no good or bad feelings. Feelings and emotions are natural reactions of the body-mind to stimuli and conditioning. There is no need to manage, understand, or change feelings. They are not indicators of progress, spiritual or otherwise. Sensations and feelings unfold spontaneously. They come and they go.

Nothing in experience itself changes due to this knowing. There may be bliss, deep spiritual experiences, or fear and frustration. The experience continues according to the conditioning of the particular body-mind. But no matter what experience is like, **You** are both all experience and what is aware of experience.

The character often remains much the same, and no one else notices a change. There will likely be a sense of *me* until death. But now our true nature is known. The quality of experience changes, not necessarily the content. Life is joyful, even in the bad, because it is impersonal. **You** know that it is not about you.

There is no need for selfing to stop. The self doesn't disappear. What disappears is the belief that *we* are the selfing, and our obsession with it. Selfing becomes less sticky and stops causing psychological turmoil. The role continues to be played. But now **You** know that the character is not what you are. Neither is anyone else! It's just life unfolding spontaneously and freely. The belief that this is about a particular experience can't be true, because all experiences come and go. Awakening is the end of the need for anything to be a particular way.

Embodying It

There's nothing to do and no one to do it. Still, thoughts appear about new practices, other paths, deepening understanding, embodying it fully, and seeing it more clearly. We may even try to create a distinction between an initial awakening and a subsequent process of embodiment.

Beliefs about embodying or living this understanding can be very sticky. There's the belief that this must be deepened or stabilized and fully expressed in our lives. Our behavior must reflect our inner realization. But who is going to stabilize? Who is going to embody? Where is the doer making the behavior happen?

The idea that we must learn to fully live this understanding still implies a separate self that must be fixed. It also implies time. *Reality is not perfect the way it is now, because some aspects of my behavior are still not good enough.* The idea that we must learn to embody this understanding is yet another version of self-improvement. But nothing in this moment requires a *you* to change it. What is can't be anything other than what it is. It's only a self that believes it should be.

Experience is always spontaneously arising and unfolding. It is constantly changing. It is exactly the way it is. If the body-mind is not living the understanding as the self believes it should, then that is what is happening. If the body continues to experience fear, to be unkind, or to judge, then that is what is occurring.

Awakening is awakening *from* the so-called person. The idea that a someone can embody something stops making sense. The freedom is that the resistance to life disappears, and we can just be lived as an apparent self. Trying to deepen or embody this is another way of resisting life. It causes suffering. The solution is always to return to inquiry and once again notice what is aware of whatever is going on.

Doubts and Setbacks

Whenever there is doubt, come back to inquiry. Whenever a thought about not getting it or having lost it comes up, inquire. **You** already are: before, during, and after any doubts.

There will be resistance to inquiry. There will be thoughts like, *I should have seen this by now—why is there still doubt?* Ignore them and come back to the basic questions: What am I? What is aware? Is there a separate self anywhere? Clear that up with inquiry. See once again that it is already doubtless.

What was seen or understood in the past is of zero use *now*. This realization is never finished, because it is not an event. It is alive. Right now, is it clear what **You** are and what you're not? That's all that ever counts. If it isn't clear, clear it up by looking and investigating.

It's only the mind that imagines setbacks. Setbacks are not possible because this is always already the case. Setbacks are just more cases of thinking and believing the thinking. Know what **You** are. It doesn't matter how long you seem to lose it—the moment you remember, **You** rediscover yourself. Certainty comes from seeing this again and again.

Sometimes we're fascinated by nondual teachings the way we are fascinated by human drama. We're looking for the next distraction from *this*, from being no thing and no one. The seeking and searching for something—*It can't be this!*—begins again, and we feel like what is here is not enough. It can seem like a setback because when we first discovered this there was a high, and now everything seems flat. But another's insights, teachings, videos, or books, no matter how deep or beautiful, will never satisfy. What satisfies is knowing the freedom that we are, right now.

Freedom to Be

What do we get from inquiry? Freedom. That's it. This is not for everyone. Most people don't want freedom—they want a better life for the person they believe they are. They want more success, happiness, love, or appreciation for a self.

The paradox is that this freedom to *be* does produce an easier and more joyful life. However, it's not a self that is now more free: it's freedom from identification with the self, leading to the freedom to be as the body-mind naturally is. We continue to experience life as a body-mind and are simultaneously free from problems and frictions because we know those things aren't what we are. We no longer need anything to be any different than it is. What ends is the belief that we're not free.

Ultimately, it's not even freedom from the self but freedom *as the self*, due to the realization that there is no self to be free! In his book *The Way of Freedom*, nonduality teacher Salvadore Poe has this to say:

> *Being finished means you know you are free, period. Seeking is over. You know you are whole and complete, lacking nothing, and there is nothing more that needs to be found or attained. Being finished means you know you are free. There can be thoughts and it won't matter because you know you are free.*

There is no liberation, awakening, or enlightenment. There is no such thing as an enlightened person. There is simply the end of the belief in separation, limitation, and bondage. There is the simple rediscovery of *this* as already fully awake and free. So we can all stop pretending that it isn't, or that we're separate from it.

This is available to anyone willing to inquire—to ignore their learned beliefs long enough to see through to naked reality. Once clearly seen, it is the most obvious thing in the world, and we realize we already knew it to be the case. We were already the sky. We were only pretending to be clouds.

Life as Ongoing Inquiry

Continue to remind yourself of what you are, even though there is no one to make that happen. Society continually interacts with you as a separate self, so reminders are needed, often for many years, as the identification with selfing slowly unwinds.

Eventually, reminders are no longer necessary, because no-self is the default. The seeming *act* of inquiring disappears, and life becomes ongoing inquiry in the sense of a simple, constant knowing of nondual Awareness even as experience remains dual. I know that *I am* and that there is no self, even when experience continues as a body-mind.

Whenever we are pulled back into identification with the separate self, sooner or later there is a spontaneous reawakening. We don't have to worry, because what has been seen cannot be unseen. More and more, we will simply know. More and more, we know ourselves as the sky that we always already were. This process does itself. There is nothing for *you* to make happen.

A spontaneous inner pause.

Thinking moves to the background.

I am already here.

Present, alive, aware.

Eternal, infinite, free.

Attention drops from selfing.

Aliveness knows itself as itself.

Identification with the body-mind drops.

Falling into this, *as* this, *there is only* this.

Consciously aware, seamless, undivided Aliveness.

Untouched freedom, ease, and joy.

Before the world appears,

You *are.*

Before the body appears,

You *are.*

Before the mind appears,

You *are.*

The One reading this doesn't have a form.

It has no limits.

It has no past or future.

It has no self or identity.

It contains no concepts.

It is not visible.

It was never born.

And it never dies.

There is a gate to freedom.

This gate is so narrow that not even a camel will fit through.

Still, everyone tries to fit their camel through the gate.

They push the poor animal, trying to squeeze it through. When that doesn't work, they attempt to starve it until it is thin enough. It never gets thin enough.

Only very few will stop trying to get their camel through the gate.

There is a narrow gate to liberation.

Once through the gate, it is seen that there is no gate. It was yet another illusion. But from this side, it looks very real.

This gate is so narrow that you can't get through it with your self.

You can't bring the separate self— the person you believe you are—into this understanding.

Index of Inquiries

Resources

The current landscape of nonduality teachings is difficult to navigate. There are different teachers endorsing various paths, there are teachers and guides who are not affiliated with any lineage at all, and there are even nonduality coaches. An additional hurdle is that no one knows what style of inquiry will work best for you. This is one reason that I do not recommend any individuals in particular.

This book recommends that you commit to your own inquiry, and it can absolutely work without any external help at all. But if you do find yourself feeling unbearably stuck, you may want to consider finding a guide to support you. There are many resources available for this. The volunteer guiding site Liberation Unleashed (*www.liberationunleashed.com*) is one place to start.

Perhaps the inquiry that speaks to you was not among those included in this book. That doesn't mean you should give up on inquiry as a direct means of waking up from the dream of self and separation. It could just mean that this author's choice of language didn't click with you.

Below is a list of books by other authors whose language may resonate more. They offer different expressions and instructions, as well as many more options for inquiry. Browse through them and see if one speaks to you.

Adyashanti. *The Direct Way: Thirty Practices to Evoke Awakening*. Sounds True, 2021.

Amery, Helen, and Sara Priestley. *The Complete Book of Awakening*. Thoughtful Raven, 2022.

Ciunaite, Ilona. *Liberation Unleashed: A Guide to Breaking Free from the Illusion of a Separate Self*. Published by the author, 2016.

Davis, Fred. *Awaken NOW: The Living Method of Spiritual Awakening*. Published by the author, 2016.

Halaw, Andre Doshim. *Neti-Neti Meditation*. Published by the author, 2013.

Poe, Salvadore. *Liberation IS: The End of the Spiritual Path*. Liberation IS Press, 2018.

———————. *The Way of Freedom: Conversations with Salvadore Poe*. Liberation IS Press, 2018.

Sefton, John. *Identifying Nonduality: A Guide to Recognizing Our True Nature.* Published by the author, 2021.

Spira, Rupert. *Being Aware of Being Aware*. Sahaja Publications, 2017.

———————. *Being Myself*. Sahaja Publications, 2021.

———————. *The Heart of Prayer*. Sahaja Publications, 2023.

Illustration Credits

Crowd graphic ©Tawng via Canva.com

Clouds graphic ©Sketchify Japan via Canva.com

Body-mind graphics designed using assets by Vectoryzen and Greenflash via Canva.com

Selfing loop graphics designed using assets by crownlab via Canva.com

Venn diagram ©Vladimir Ivankin via Canva.com

Scribbled head illustration ©Pavlo Kravchenko via Canva.com

Paradox shape ©WinWin.artlab via Canva.com

What we are/not chart designed using assets by Kozy Place, MariaLevArt, Atstock Productions, WEBTECHOPS LLP, Kelly's Images, and Anna Hirna via Canva.com

Spiral chart designed using graphics by Yaroslav Matveev via Canva.com

About the Author

Katrijn Van Oudheusden writes about recognizing our true, nondual nature by seeing through the illusion of the self. Originally from Belgium, she was raised in Thailand and had a twenty-year career in law and organizational development in the Netherlands and Germany. She now lives in Frankfurt with her husband. In addition to writing books on nonduality, she shares free weekly reflections on our self-less nature via her Daily Nonduality newsletter. Visit her at *katoudheusden.com*.

Hierophant publishing
books that inspire your body, mind, and spirit
San Antonio, TX
www.hierophantpublishing.com